"This mini-beauty course of ABC requirements for enhancing outward beauty is very basic, but it might mean the difference between confirming and denying the faith that is within you.

"It would be wonderful if we could stand at a distance and see ourselves as God and men see us. Maybe we would immediately be able to properly evaluate our looks.

"But all we really have is God's mirror (His Word) for our faith and our dressing room mirror for our face. Let's use them both enthusiastically to be the beautiful women of faith and face God intended."
—JOYCE LANDORF

While this book is designed for reading enjoyment and individual instruction, it also is intended for use as a book for group study. A leader's guide is available at $1.25 from your local bookstore or from the publisher.

P9-DFY-462

JOYCE LANDORF, radiant beauty, is both a home-maker and a career woman. She is a singer who has recorded several albums—"Peace Through the Lord," "It's Great To Be Alive," and her newest, "Joyce." Joyce is the recipient of numerous Outstanding Service Awards from the U.S. Military for appearances around the world. Singing and speaking at churches, women's clubs, Family Forums, and other gatherings—all keep Joyce on the go. She is author of *Let's Have a Banquet, His Stubborn Love, To Lib or Not To Lib, The Richest Lady in Town, Mourning Song,* and *Mix with Love,* and writes a column for *Power For Living,* published by Scripture Press.

THE FRAGRANCE
OF BEAUTY

Joyce Landorf

VICTOR BOOKS

a division of SP Publications, Inc., Wheaton, Illinois

Offices also in Fullerton, California • Whitby, Ontario, Canada • London, England

Unless otherwise indicated, Scripture quotations are from the *Living Bible*. Other quotations are from the authorized version (KJV), and from the *New Testament in Modern English* by J. B. Phillips (PH), used by permission.

THE FRAGRANCE OF BEAUTY

Published by Victor Books, a Division of SP Publications, Inc., P.O. Box 1825, Wheaton, Ill. 60187

Seventeenth printing, 1979

ISBN 0-88207-231-5

Library of Congress Catalog Card Number 73—76813

To: A Woman
Who gave herself totally to Christ,
Who was granted freedom by God's forgiveness,
Who has dropped her insecurities, hang-ups, and
  fears at the Cross,
  and
Who now walks with her head held high,
  in the sunshine of God's love
  and is surrounded by the
  incredible fragrance of His beauty:
                    Clare Bauer

The Fragrance of Beauty

CONTENTS

CHAPTER ONE

MAN CERTAINLY DOES LOOK ON THE OUTSIDE!

Just a few years ago, a minister's wife, Perky Brandt, shared her concern with me over the women in her church.

"They come in all shapes, sizes, and ages," she said, "but somehow they share a common look." My concerned friend had a difficult time putting it into words, but suddenly she said, "It has something to do with their lack of inner beauty, and it seems to affect their outer looks too. Do you suppose as Christian women we need some kind of a charm or self-improvement course?"

My immediate reaction was a quick no. I reasoned that Christian women didn't need *any* courses, books, or lessons on beauty. After all, when a woman truly accepts Christ, the Creator of all beauty, as her Saviour, isn't she as radiant as a bride? Isn't she beautiful, just knowing she's loved and allowing the Lord Himself to shine through her?

But my next thought was, "Or is she?"

My many speaking and singing engagements provided the perfect opportunity for taking a good look at Christian women. Before I tell you what I found, I must make one thing clear. I deplore, not only in our society, but in the whole world the continual, incessant worship of beauty and youth. All you need is one flaw, one physical or emotional defect, and you cannot qualify for the beautiful-people set.

There is not a line in this writing intended to give support to an already over-worshiped beauty cult. Rather, I pray this book will help us to take a good look at today's woman. Then, perhaps we can sanely evaluate all our vital statistics in their proper relationship to our lives and discover ways to be at our very best.

When I began to take a purely academic look at my audiences, at the women in my own church, and yes, even at myself, I did see a need.

Later in this book I want to develop some of the how's and why's of inner beauty, but first let me tell you what I saw on the outside of Christian women.

I started with the teen-age girl. I live with one fantastic specimen, our daughter Laurie, and true to form for most teen-agers, she almost dies if she doesn't look *exactly* like everyone else at school. (Don't frown, Mother, remember each generation wears their own things. The sloppy Joe sweaters of the 40s, the sweater sets of the 50s, the jeans of the 60s, and the layered look of the 70s are examples.) Nevertheless, I saw far more need to develop positive feelings of self-worth than I did to develop skills for facial make-up, for example, because those "emotional" teen years can be pretty painful. At this point, however, I was not looking inwardly—just concentrating on the outward impressions. While most teen girls had no idea what makeup was best for their facial shape or coloring, observation told me they readily accepted the concept of *doing something* about their physical appearance.

Then my eye fell on some teen-aged girls who were so turned off by the beauty-worship rituals of our society that they had gone as far as they could in the opposite direction. To be as plain, as ugly, as unbeautiful as possible seemed to be their goal. In view of the continual stress on the need to be beautiful, I understood their rebellion, though I do not agree with it.

The next age group I studied—the 25-35-year-old married women—was the most divided in looks. Most of them were mothers of babies and/or very young children. About half the group were sparkling and vivacious. They seemed to have left their ugly, awkward stages completely behind. Their faces were alive with individualized beauty. Their clothing, makeup, and poise seemed excellent.

The other half were a different story. They lacked the luster and glow of their peer group. Their general attitude toward clothes, makeup, and poise seemed to be one of apathy or just plain carelessness. Fatigue, depression, and lack of self-worth seemed to be written across their lives, showing in their posture and the way they walked. The way one young mother brought a coldness into a room and then slumped heavily down in her chair presented a fairly accurate picture of the tone of her life.

The 35- to 50-year-olds were the most interesting. At an age when they should have matured out of earlier inferiority complexes, many seemed to be wallowing in them. Their children were older and less demanding, and fatigue should not have been such a problem. Yet, boredom showed in their faces. Now, when they could afford cosmetics, haircuts, and at least occasional visits to the hairdresser, their looks needed the most help. Skin and hair problems were quite evident. The flabbiness and shape of their figures told me they had neglected one of the best techniques of preventive medicine: exercise.

I had long carried a mental image of the typical Christian woman as one who might be plain-featured, but one who, because of Christ's inner glow radiating from her heart to her face, is beautiful, all in her own special way. But where were these beautiful-in-Christ women I was hoping to find? Why, in my looking, had I not seen many such beautiful women? Had it always been like this?

I searched my memory, back to 30 years ago, when I was 10. The women of our church were instantly recognizable then. I wish I could say they were recognizable because of love, joy, and the beauty of Christ, but that was simply not true in most cases.

If three pagan women and one Christian woman were waiting for a bus at the corner, you could instantly tell which one was the Christian. She was always the perfectly dreadful looking one.

She prided herself on the alleged fact that she wore no makeup. I say "alleged" because she usually broke form to apply a colorless layer of powder. Her hair was rarely cut, and usually it was pulled tightly back into a small bun. Sometimes it was just left hanging and bobby pinned on the sides. Her dress was always a somber, dreary navy or black number in a "sensible" style of some year long past.

But while the Christian woman looked like quite a misfit at the bus stop, in church circles it was a different story. She was considered "very spiritual." (I used to think, "Yes, ugly, but definitely spiritual.")

For a time, my own mother was caught in this trap and felt that you had to *look* spiritual in order to *be* spiritual. I guess nobody had come up with the theory that if you *are* spiritual you will *look* spiritual. They continued putting the cart before the horse.

My mother "copped out" once in awhile, and I particularly remember a navy blue dress that was completely embroidered with tiny red and yellow flowers and bright kelly green leaves. I loved her in it. The ladies in my father's church, however, felt she had lost a great deal of her spiritual depth, and they graciously made the whole thing a matter of discussion and prayer at the next Ladies' Missionary Society meeting. Much to my delight, Mother wore it anyway the following Sunday. Actually, she continued to rather gleefully wear it until finally the ladies began questioning my *father's* spirituality. After that, the dress disappeared into a chest, and some months later I got it to use as a dress-up play dress.

Anyway, in those days it was safe to assume that most Christian women were not glowingly beautiful. I feel all that was changed by a very imaginative woman who came along in the 30s: Aimee Semple McPherson, a woman preacher in Los Angeles, Calif.

She exploded on the church scene as we knew it with a flamboyance that astounded everyone. Her

fame reached from California to the little town in Ontario, Canada, where I lived, and people talked about
her. My, *how* they talked about her!

First it was rumored, and then positively reported,
"Aimee wore makeup to church." Whether you agreed
with her theology or not, you had to admit she could
sing and preach, and she looked extremely beautiful
while doing it. Such a phenomenon! We were all
stunned in our little Canadian town, and you should
have heard the discussion and prayer time at the Ladies' Missionary Meeting that week.

When Aimee preached in elegant evening gowns,
we were all properly shocked (again). When she took
the hottest fashion garments of the day, capes, and
dressed her choir and usherettes in them, most of us
felt that was the last straw of worldliness. But Aimee
went on and on.

Evidently Aimee was also depressed over the
dreary, ugly church auditoriums of those days, for she
helped design one of the most beautiful sanctuaries
anyone had seen, even in the free-wheeling West. (It
was shockingly similar to a theater and quite a depar-
ture for a church.)

Beauty—outward beauty—came to church, and
Aimee Semple McPherson, was certainly responsible
for that trend. Her beautiful auditorium not only became the scene for illustrated sermons, but was one
of the first to have a full orchestra and a complete
band. Christian musicals, operas, and dramas were
presented on her stage, and she herself seemed to say,
"Women, you don't have to be ugly and plain to prove
how spiritual you are. Actually, you have absolutely
the biggest potential of all women to be creatively and
positively beautiful—inwardly *and outwardly!*"

In Christian circles today, the percentage of lovely,
attractive, beautifully groomed women has certainly
come way up from those days in the 30s. There is a
definite decline in the number of old-hold-outs trying
to "look spiritual," and for this I'm grateful. But what
disturbed my friend Perky and subsequently aroused

me was the large segment of Christian women who, while they were dressed neatly and modestly, still had the drab, worn-out-bathrobe look. They could have been vastly more attractive in other areas—hair, skin, figure, posture, and poise, but many were not doing anything about using what they had. I saw so much unused potential.

Patricia French, the dazzling beauty who is the founder and director of the only Christian charm and modeling school I know of, said, "So many times the average Christian woman of today wants to be so 'spiritual' that she has lost her prettiness, her natural flair for beauty. In fact, she is *so* basic she's boring."

I personally wish with all my heart that that statement were not accurate, but I'm afraid it is. The key words in it are "lost . . . her natural flair for beauty" and "she is . . . boring."

After I had shared the results of my survey of the feminine beauty scene with Perky, we outlined a program for the women of her church called *GLO*. It called for three morning sessions starting with a 9:00 A.M. coffee and then classes from 9:30 to noon. The women would bring sack lunches, and a nursery would be provided.

The first session would be on *Glamour*. It would include a very general, basic course on make-up, skin care, and hair treatment. The next session would be on *Living*. I would bring about 20 handmade items from my home. Some were simple, but all were very practical. I made many things from ideas found in magazines. Others I made after I'd taken a night course in the local high school. We would talk about developing skills in homemaking and the value it adds to our own personal estimation of our self-worth. We would also discuss eating and dressing on a small salary. The last session would be called *Opportunity*. I would give my personal testimony and outline the process by which God inwardly transforms ugliness into His loveliness. I would also describe some of the destructive things that rob any woman, Christian or not, of the priceless commodity called inner beauty.

Together, Perky and I set all this down on paper. Then she told the church women about the proposed series. Before we could even set a date to begin, we got the first negative feedback. It seemed that some of the older ladies, reverting to the days of "looking spiritual," felt that we must remember man looketh on the outside but God looketh on the inside. They felt we should concern ourselves only with inner beauty and not dwell on outward apperance at all. But really, wasn't 1 Peter 3:3 clear on that point? "Whose adorning let it not be that outward adorning of plaiting the hair, and of wearing of gold, or of putting on of apparel." (KJV).

When I heard this, I had to smile, because that very week a bedraggled, tousled Christian woman (who hadn't even bothered to comb her hair) had sat in my living room and with a voice full of self-pity whined, "I just can't figure it out! I've been a faithful wife, a good cook, a good mother to our children, but my husband never looks at me any more, and he never says 'I love you.' I just don't understand it!"

I thought, "You're wrong about your husband never looking at you. Actually, your husband *has* looked at you, and when he caught a glimpse of your Phyllis Diller hairdo and Mama Cass figure, he didn't feel he wanted to look any farther. He didn't have any incentive to express his love, and he certainly was handicapped in trying to see what God might see in you."

It is true that God beholds our inner beauty, inner motives, inner thoughts and dreams, but man has *nowhere else to look* but on the outward appearance! Remember that.

When a man sees a woman, he looks first at her physical qualifications. It's a built-in natural trait with him. He'll look at her face and her figure, but not necessarily in that order. Then, if a woman has those marvelous inner qualities that are of God, the man will see the shining reflection of God. The physical and inner looks blend into one picture, and the total woman comes into focus. The entire scene in his mind becomes one of pure joy. The woman is warm, giving, alert, fun to be with, loving, and, yes, spiritual, but she also has an earthly sexiness that is uncommonly beautiful, and all he can say is, "Wow!"

But what about Peter's warning against outward adorning? The fact is that we women *can* get a little carried away with the pursuit of "beauty." Peter saw the fantastic dangers in that practice and was warning Christian women not to be *overly concerned* about what they wore nor overly occupied with their outward adornments to the neglect of the far more important inner beauty. The key words here are "overly concerned." I am confident that is what Peter meant, for if we carried out his words to their literal end, they would require that women go nude. "Whose adorning let it not be that of . . . putting on of apparel."

I can take Peter's gentle warning in the best of spirits because he really endears himself to me when, in that same chapter, he tells the husbands to be careful how they treat their wives, who are *"partners"* in receiving God's blessings." (That must have been quite a news bulletin in that age of male dominance!) Then he says, "And if you don't treat her as you should, your prayers will not get ready answers" (1 Peter 3:7).

The need in Perky's church still existed, so after we'd examined these and other Scriptures on beauty, and after we had prayed and talked, we enthusiastically decided to go ahead with the GLO series in spite of the negative feedback.

The success was marvelous, and even though this happened several years ago, I'm still reminded of it periodically by someone who attended. Last week, as I was shopping in our local grocery store, a woman came up the aisle. We chatted briefly, and since she really did look lovely, I said so. She thanked me and then added, "You know, every time I get ready to come to the market, I remember what you said in the GLO series about Christian women in hair curlers and rollers in public, and I stop and take special pains to see that my hair is combed and brushed." Then she added, "And I feel so special." She looked it, too.

I'm sure our husbands don't expect our figures and faces to rival those of some Hollywood sexpot. But from talking to a great many men in researching this book, I've found they would like us to do more with the assets we have. It seems men want a girl to look like a *girl!* The men who responded to my question, "What trait would you want to change in your wife?" seemed with one voice to say, "She should be more woman, inside and out."

After warning women about being concerned with beauty that *depends* on jewelry, clothes, or hair arrangement, Peter says, "Be beautiful inside, in your hearts, with the lasting charm of a gentle and quiet spirit which is so precious to God" (1 Peter 3:4).

A gentle and quiet spirit is not only precious to God, but to men as well. That's what charm and beauty are all about—not getting too wrapped up in the outward, yet not ignoring it either, but striving for that incredible shining, inner beauty that truly outglows any other kind. It's making the best of the original you that God designed and created.

Once my mother-in-law and I had lunch in the fashionable tearoom of Bullock's Department Store. It turned out to be more of a treat than we guessed because along with lunch came a fantastic designer's fashion show. The clothes were simply elegance personified, and all the models were rare examples of pure beauty. One, however, outshone all of them. She had only to set one toe through the stage curtain and we found ourselves wildly applauding! If she had come on stage in a burlap sack, we would have still thought her exquisite! She was a beautiful collection of God's finest handiwork from her shining, alive-looking hair and her peaches and cream complexion, down to her flawless figure and perfectly sculptured legs. And she was the hit of the show.

Long after lunch we were still talking about her.

Then we saw three of the models from the show waiting at the end of a counter, and it wasn't long until we knew who they were waiting for. Flying across the store, leaving a trail of staring people behind her, came this gorgeous model.

Once again we were awestruck by her incredible beauty—but only briefly, for even before she reached her friends, her mouth opened and out poured a barrage of the most filthy, critical, and angry language we'd ever heard. She was furious at the fashion coordinator, the clothes, the time limit, and a certain "blonde" who she felt had stolen the show from her. It was while I was absorbed in all this that I realized my eyes were doing strange things. The longer that beautiful model talked and the longer I watched, the more she began to change right before my eyes.

The brilliant, dancing lights in her hair dulled. Her eyelashes, once long black sweeps of beauty, grew shorter and shorter and became ugly stumps. Her skin showed red blotches, scars from a latent teen-age case of acne seemed to appear, and her hips began to thicken. Her once slim ankles looked exactly as mine had when I was nine months pregnant with Laurie and retaining all fluids. In short, before my very eyes, the most beautifully endowed woman I'd ever seen became ugly, as all her outward beauty was lost in the vile outpouring of her soul.

Evidently we need to develop areas of beauty—outer and inner. But what really is true beauty?

True beauty is latent in all women. Some are blessed of God with truly great outward and inner beauty both. But most women I know have a certain *quality* of beauty rather than a whole suitcase of it. Truly wise is the woman who accurately perceives both her good features and her weak traits and does the most with what she's got.

I invite you, here and now, to examine the claims of Christ, the Originator of all beauty, for without Him one hasn't a chance of remaining beautiful inside or out. Without Him, you could look like a beautiful model at Bullock's and still be ugly. With Him, you could have a very "plain Jane" face and yet display a deep and lasting beauty.

I'm writing this with the prayer that the fragrance of God's beauty will enfold and surround your entire being. Being beautiful in Jesus very definitely involves both our inner soul's condition and our outward appearance. One confirms or denies the other. They are both important. Neither must be slighted.

While I'm sure Paul was not considered a beauty expert in his day, he nevertheless has set down a statement about our lives as Christians that may be particularly applied to our beauty as women.

"But thanks be to God! For through what Christ has done, He has triumphed over us so that now wherever we go, He uses us to tell others about the Lord and to spread the Gospel like a sweet perfume. As far as God is concerned there is a sweet wholesome fragrance in our lives. It is the fragrance of Christ within us, an aroma of both the saved and the unsaved all around us" (2 Cor. 2:14, 15).

It is true, as the next verse points out, that not everyone will appreciate our fragrant beauty no matter how Christlike and outwardly attractive we may be. The very fragrance of our life in Christ may be a smell of death to some, because they don't want Christ.

In this sense the familiar saying, "Beauty is in the eye of the beholder," finds its deepest and most profound validation. Even the altogether lovely Christ "hath no form nor comeliness and . . . no beauty that we should desire Him" to those who love their sins, (Isa. 53:2, KJV).

In any case, we are being watched. Our lives do speak to others. The beauty of Christ ought to shine forth. Let's examine our inner selves and our outward looks and determine exactly what fragrance is going forth.

"If a woman's soul is without cultivation, without

taste, without refinement, without sweetness of a happy mind, not all the mysteries of art can ever make her face beautiful. . . . I find no art which can atone for an unpolished mind and an unlovely heart.*

CHAPTER TWO

FEAR: A ROARING LION

There are several inner conflicts that can plunder and rob a woman of her natural beauty.

The chief criminal of these inner conflicts is FEAR.

A woman can be beautifully coiffured, expertly made up, and properly groomed; yet, if fear has vandalized her soul, then her face, her walk, and her words will betray her. Nothing she can do will disguise the disastrous results of fear.

In one of my mother's notebooks I found these descriptive lines:

Where Worry is a mouse,
a small scampering thing with sharp tiny feet,
that scurries over our souls—
Fear is a roaring lion,
with huge paws, extended claws and teeth
that slash us into strips.

I've seen this lion at work, tearing, maiming, roaring, and paralyzing all movement, not only in my life but in the lives of many women. We are all at one time or another the lion's victim.

A tense young woman nervously understates, "I'm afraid my marriage is over."

*From *The Arts and Secrets of Beauty* by Madame Lola Montez, 1853, Chelsea House Publishers, New York, N.Y., 1969.

A bank teller honestly faces up to a fact when she says, "My only fear is the fear of death."

A distraught young wife, biting at the edge of what was once a fingernail says, "My husband has been out of work for months; we may have to go into bankruptcy. There is no financial security left any more and I'm afraid. I'm scared to death."

A wife, barely able to control her ravaged emotions, trembles as she blurts out, "My worst fears have come true. What I've suspected for years is now confirmed. My husband says he's never loved me, that he's 'gay,' a practicing homosexual, and he's leaving me. What will I do? I'm so afraid."

A mother, admitting a fear that has become a reality for the first time, whispers, "My son is on drugs. I am filled with fear."

A young bride thinks it's silly of her, yet she confesses, "Every time Ron is even a little late from work, I just know he has been in an accident, is hurt, or worse—is dead."

An older woman remembers her childhood and reminisces, "If I came home from school and nobody was there, I'd always be scared to death that the Lord had come back and I'd been left behind."

A teen-age girl, twisting with the weight of an enormous guilt, stammers, "I'm afraid I'm going to have a baby."

These fears have been expressed to me—brought into the open where we could examine them. But for every shared fear, there are probably many unspoken fears, hidden fears, even unacknowledged fears, that lie just under the surface of many a woman's face.

All of these women, with their different fears, shared the same look. The same panic and the same destruction was written across their faces. Fear is powerful. It is a panic in the blood, and it attacks the heart.

David wrote, "My heart is in anguish within me. Stark fear overpowers me" (Ps. 55:4). Fear can cause complete blockage to one's normal, rational thinking and it is an emotion which can paralyze all movement. David expertly diagnosed fear when he wrote, "I am losing all hope; I am paralyzed with fear" (Ps. 143:4).

It is entirely possible to be a child of God (or even the King of Israel) and experience the stark power of fear. I do not want to give the impression that Christians should never have any fear. That's simply not true. We are all susceptible to fear that flashes its lightning at us.

When a doctor says to me, "Mrs. Landorf, I don't mean to alarm you; however, we have found . . ."

I'll tell you *I am alarmed*—before he even finishes the sentence! That I am struck with fear is a fact of life. But I will not be paralyzed by this fear if I remember God can be trusted.

Eugenia Price, writing in *Just As I Am,** states:

> I grow afraid, just as you do. But my fear, even of the death of a loved one (most difficult of all for me), lives and grows only as long as I turn to other people with it; only as long as I try to overcome it myself. It is cast out (the unhealthy, destructive fear—not the circumstance) when I deliberately remember Jesus.

The woman who lets the roaring lion of fear take over in her world will show this fear first in her walk and arm movements; then in her face. Consider this hypothetical Christian woman. She has just heard her doctor diagnose her problem as "breast cancer." She cannot move. Her previous anxiety and general feeling of apprehension has now changed to fear. She is in a stunned, paralyzed position. She denies the truth of it even as she listens to her concerned doctor. When she finally tries to leave his office, she finds she's severely limited in her ability to walk. She has become rather uncoordinated and the simple act of walking across a room has become a monumental chore. She reaches for the door handle but misses on the first try.

*Zondervan Publishing House, Grand Rapids, Mich.

Still in shock, she finds herself becoming rigid and harsh. She drives home and tries to pull herself together to tell her family. If the fear is great enough she will wait hours or days. In any case, by the time she has regained enough courage to tell them, the family already knows something is seriously wrong. After that her every waking moment is filled with fearful thoughts. She forgets Jesus. She allows herself to be mauled by the lion of fear. She eventually closes her mind against surgery or refuses to change her opinion about some other treatment. Her mind seems to refuse to think logically or move in any direction.

If her fear is of a less serious threat than cancer, if she fears driving on the freeway or flying in a jet, she will not get into a car and she will not board a jet. Her whole life hardens into a steel-reinforced rut.

Seneca makes the wife of Hercules say of Lyches, "His mind is like he walks." When fear grips our lives, every move reflects it.

One of the first ingredients of beauty and graciousness in a woman is a cool, relaxed, prepared look. The woman of true beauty usually looks as if she can calmly handle anything from a house afire to a spilt glass of milk on her carpeting.

This prerequisite of charm is completely obliterated by the lion of fear.

Then, look at what fear does to a woman's face.

Just as fear restricts any relaxed movement and paralyzes the mind and body, it also hardens facial expressions into frozen masks. If a woman's fear is great, she rarely finds anything to smile about, and all others see is a cold, rather sterile countenance. Nothing makes it light up in expectation and nothing softens the almost-a-frown expression. And nothing ages a face quite so fast as fear.

Perhaps none of the fears I've already mentioned have attacked you, but here are some other fears women have disclosed to me. Some are major threats; others are rather trivial; but all are real fears. Do some of these sound distressingly familiar?

The fear of . . .

1. Wondering what others (my husband, mother-in-law, neighbor, boss, peers) will say or think.
2. Traveling, driving, or flying alone.
3. Discovering cancer in any degree or quantity.
4. Dying.
5. Being a widow.
6. Losing a child either to drugs, alcohol, or disease.
7. Not having anyone left to love or need you.
8. Suspecting your husband is having an extra-marital affair.
9. Failing (at marriage, raising children, on the job, or with some responsibility).
10. Being disappointed in people *again*.
11. Bankruptcy.
12. Seeing a live snake, lizard, and/or spiders.
13. Growing old ungracefully.
14. Being left alone and isolated from family and friends.
15. Pregnancy.
16. Being caught in an immoral or illegal act.
17. Being physically or sexually inadequate in marriage.
18. Dealing with problems or conflicts.
19. Change.
20. Making a decision.

I've left space here for you to add your own special fears and I encourage you to compile your personal list with directness and objective honesty. After you've added your own fears, then go back over my list and check any there that are apparent in your life—no matter how large or slight the fear may be.

It is very important now to carefully study your list because there are two main things we love to do with our fears. One is to deny their very existence. The second is to run away from them as fast as our little minds can carry us—looking frantically for a place to hide from the lion.

After David admits that "stark" fear has overpowered him, he goes on to say, "I would fly to the far off deserts and stay there. I would flee to some refuge from all this storm" (Ps. 55:6-8).

His desire to run and hide from his fears has an all too familiar ring to it.

There seems to be an ostrichlike quality about the way people run or hide from fears, and no end to the ways in which they fantasize about them.

They turn to alcohol and drink too much.

They try taking tranquilizers, sleeping tablets, and pep pills.

They go to bed with a pseudo or psychosomatic illness.

They spend much time analyzing their childhood miseries.

They sit for hours with glazed eyes before a television set.

They go on a reading kick and read one book after another.

They flirt with the opposite sex.

They concentrate all their efforts on making money.

They develop compulsive buying habits.

They join one organization after another.

They develop all sorts of mental mechanisms which prevent them from recognizing the basic problems within—all in the frantic effort to drown out the roaring of the lion of fear.

New techniques of escape are constantly being developed. New medicines are flooding the market to enable us to endure this fearful modern world in which we live.

"But how in the world can I cope with these personal fears?" you ask. If you've honestly and realistically listed your fears—big ones and little ones—you've already taken the first step in dealing with the lion. Jesus never said we'd be exempt from having problems and fears. In fact, He said we would have trouble (cf John 16:33).

Psychologists and doctors agree that until you find out what ails you, you cannot be cured. Mental health begins by admitting and then accepting, all the facts of our lives—including the unpleasant, the conflicting, or the ugly situations.

The second step in coping with fear is found in asking, "Who is the author of fear?"

It is not enough to honestly pinpoint our fear. We must find out where it originates and stop it at the source.

God does not give fear.

"For God hath not given us the spirit of fear" (2 Tim. 1:7, KJV). Our Bible explicity states that God is love . . . and that perfect love casts out all fear (see 1 John 4:8, 18).

Paul observes the Christians in Galatia and questions, "You were getting along so well. Who has interfered with you to hold you back from following the truth? It certainly isn't God who has done it, for He is the one who has called you to freedom in Christ" (Gal. 5:7).

When you hear the first little ping of fearful thought sound off in your brain, remember instantly that it is not from God!

Hal Lindsey, in his brilliant but scary book, *Satan Is Alive and Well on Planet Earth,* gives superintelligent Satan the credit for inventing the power of suggestion, and he brands it as the cleverest of ways to attack us.

Satan knows the full name and social security number of every born-again Christian, and he has written it very carefully down in his book of books.

He is acutely aware that he cannot take Christ away from us or steal our salvation like a pickpocket in a crowd, but he will do his best to neutralize us into defeated, fatigued, ugly specimens of Christianity.

He finds our particular panic button and presses it for all he's worth. Your fear might be the big one about breast cancer or a little one like being afraid of driving on busy freeways but he'll find it and make it his biggest weapon for damaging your sound mental health, confident outward composure, and victorious Christian living.

His pressing our fear button rallies us to fight. So we jump up and make all kinds of New Year's resolutions. We turn over all sorts of new leaves and really make a determined effort to win. Without asking God's help, without realizing the Holy Spirit could be in control of our lives, we spin our wheels and drive in endless, fruitless circles.

This is exactly what Satan wants. In fact, it fits in perfectly with his battle plan. He wants us to think we live and fight alone, completely alone.

He plants a fear (sometimes only the suggestion of a fear), and sits back and watches us wear ourselves to a frazzle fighting it! We are an easy victory for him, particularly if he can get us to spend all our waking, and most of our sleeping, hours troubled with the fear of today or tomorrow. Don't let him rob you of one of your most priceless possessions: time.

Remember, too Satan used Scripture to tempt even Jesus so you'll be no exception to his rule. He twisted God's words to Eve in the very beginning of time, and she fell for it.

How can you tell the difference between Satan's suggestions and God's? Here's a basic rule of thumb:
If the thought is
    honest—not scrambled in any way
    pure—no ulterior motives
    kind and good—not destructive
it is almost always from the Lord. However if the thought is

  a lie—even a little white one
  a deception—the truth twisted ever so slightly
  a destructive suggestion—that will hurt
it is probably a "popped-in-suggestion" from Satan.

When I've been attacked by the lion of fear during the last few years, I've phoned my friend, Clare. She is wise in the things of God, perceptive, and never, even in the face of panic-filled times, seems to lose her God-given sense of humor.

I'll phone and say, "Clare, could I have some of your time and share my fear and panic about such and such?"

"Yes—" comes back the answer, "but only 30 seconds of panic, OK?"

The Lord knows we will have all kinds of anxieties and fears, but maybe we ought to think more in terms of dwelling on them for 30 seconds only. God's got better things for your time than your stewing, fighting, and hassling over those fears. Don't let Satan snag you on this point.

The third step in coping with our fears is determined by who we let control our lives. It always comes down to a matter of the will. *You* decide.

Paul talks of people who are still under the control of their old sinful natures. He says they can never please God. Then he talks to the new Christians and joyously announces, "But you are not like that. You are controlled by your new nature if you have the Spirit of God living in you" (Rom. 8:9).

The right answers to living with our fears are found within our own souls. The secret of victory and of having God's fragrant beauty in our lives and on our faces is not to be found in our struggling alone but in our willing surrender to Christ of the fear that gnaws at us. By using our wills, we can decide who controls, who dominates, and who wins: Satan or Christ.

If your husband or child is late getting home from school or work and you begin to get anxious about their safety and well-being, tell that to the Lord. Then commit that husband or child to Him. You can be sure of this: if God is going to do the big thing we fear at a time like this (death by some kind of accident), He will not take our loved one home one minute sooner or later than He decides. Their lives and times are in God's hands. He is in control of the universe. Don't let Satan blow your mind with false fears and imagined tragedies.

Peter vividly warns us about the enemy that would control and destroy us when he states, "Be careful, watch out for attacks from Satan, your great enemy. He prowls around like a hungry, roaring lion looking for some victim to tear apart. Stand firm when he attacks" (1 Peter 5:8).

I think the Lord would have us learn a lesson on trusting God and committing to Him our fears from Daniel. Remember him? He was the man who was thrown into a den full of roaring, hungry lions. When anyone else was thrown down, the hungry lions ate them before they even hit the bottom of the den (Dan. 6:24). Now *that* was a very real fear Daniel faced! Yet, he was so convinced his life and times were in God's hands that he decided to trust and commit this life-and-death fear to his all-seeing, all-caring God. So God did take over.

What astounds me most about this story is the thought that when Daniel was with those lions, he should have been absolutely paralyzed with fear. Yet, he was so relaxed, he probably went to sleep. The next morning, Scripture tells us, "Not a scratch was found on him because he believed in His God" (Dan. 6:23).

The lion of fear need not vandalize your inner beauty, destroy the mobility of your system, or harden the lines on your face. Take these three steps in regard to fear and you'll be closer to the beautiful, glowing woman God would have you be.

1. Spread your fears honestly before the Lord on a list and leave the list with Him. Select a shelf or table. Put your daily fears on it. Leave it alone. Stand back and let the Lord be the keeper of the shelf. The next day, when you want to think about that fear,

don't go to the shelf; don't take it down and hold it. It doesn't belong to you now. Let the Lord have it.

2. Know your enemy is Satan. He is the author of all fearful thoughts. God did not remind you of your fear. Satan did, and he'll continue to use the power of suggestion if you let him.

3. Decide exactly who you will allow to control your mind, soul, and body. The Word of God reminds us that, "Greater is He that is in you than he that is in the world" (1 John 4:4, KJV). So remember, Satan is not in first place. Jesus knows the exact depth and width of each Satan-inspired fear.

If Christ is your Lord and Saviour, then He can be trusted. He is able. Take heart. All things *will* work together for good (Rom. 8:28) even if you can't see it or figure it out right here and now. God—not Satan—is in control. He can give you all the strength and energy you'll ever need in combating the fears of a broken world. You'll come out like Daniel—not a lion's scratch to be found!

Additional references for this chapter.

Satan:	Ephesians 6:10-17
	1 John 5:19
	James 4:7
Fear:	Psalm 71:20
	Psalm 49:5
	Psalm 62:6
	1 Peter 5:7
Obedience:	James 4:17
	Joshua 1:9
Inner Beauty:	John 14:27
	John 16:33
	Psalm 94:19
	Psalm 46:1-2
	1 Peter 1:2

CHAPTER THREE

FADELESS BEAUTY OF FAITH AND FACE

If you gave your fears to Christ, as I described in the previous chapter, you are on your way to achieving the beauty of Christ!

However, it's a fact of life that when we take something out or away from our lives we leave a hole, a space, or a vacancy. We need something to replace the emptiness. What do you think the divine replacement for *fear* is? I'm sure that it's a positive working *faith*.

Fear is one of the most destructive emotions in the world. It can spread from neighbor to neighbor, mate to mate, parents to children quicker than the black plague, but so can *faith!* Beautiful faith, even tiny underdeveloped faith, can move mountains, can spread peace, can give a glimpse of hope to all whom it touches.

Fear is based on the unknown—what we think might happen. It is possible to have today's fears all safely tucked away in God's steady hand, but what about tomorrow's catastrophic fears? Faith can cover tomorrow too!

"Faith," the writer of Hebrews says, "is the confident assurance that something we want is going to happen. It is the certainty that what we hope for is waiting for us, even though we cannot see it up ahead" (Heb. 11:1).

I think it's virtually impossible to say we are believing in God fully with the realities of faith and still live in a continual state of fear.

Fear hovers in some Christian women like a low-grade fever. This "fever" is never high enough to hospitalize them, but they always have the flush of fear just under the surface.

God and prolonged fear are totally incompatible. Fear and faith are at opposite ends of the pole. A woman of faith cannot be a woman of fear.

The woman of fear will see her future as a frightening menace. She will end up afraid of her own shadow. The woman of faith, on the other hand, believes that while she may not understand all the intricate workings of God in her problems and trouble, she can view her future with confidence and hope. Whether her faith is brand new and mustard seed-sized, or older and fills a suitcase, she knows, "Anything is possible if you have faith" (Mark 9:23).

I always flinch a little when I hear a Christian woman say, "I'm so afraid of what will happen next," then almost sheepishly add, "I guess I need more faith."

Paul tells us, "God hath dealt to every man the measure of faith" (Rom. 12:3, KJV). What we need is not more faith but to use what we have! Our potential for faith is limitless.

When the Bible talks about faith, one of the clearest concepts involves our coming to Christ *just as we are* —bringing to Him our doubts, our confusion, our failures, and, yes, our fears. God cannot lie. He is the Good News. He is real, and He, so long ago, chose to love us first. Read it in Ephesians 1:4.

Faith in Christ is not a human trait like courage or trustworthiness. It's not even an attitude of heart or a state of mind which some women have while others do not. It is a supernatural phenomenon that comes in varying degrees after we have heard about Jesus, the Good News.

Paul says, "Yet faith comes from listening to this Good News—the Good News about Christ" (Rom. 10:17).

We can never please God without faith and "without depending on Him" as Hebrews 11:6 adds.

Previously I stated that fear paralyzes us. It robs us

of relaxation and poise. Faith works with exactly the opposite effect. Faith in Jesus restores the calmness of mind our body needs. It unties knotted nerves above the tummy area and loosens those tense back muscles. Faith allows you to lie down in safety and assures you a good night's rest, even though fears often loom larger at night.

Faith enables you to pray before falling asleep:
"Lord, I give You my cluttered conscious mind—it's fears and joys, its failures and successes. Here it is for You to take and hold. Now I give You my subconscious mind. You know I've no control over the passing patterns of thought or the dreams I might dream tonight, but You made me, and I will trust You. I go to sleep safe in Your keeping. Good night, dear Lord."

Our daughter, Laurie, was just about nine years old when her fear of spiders really took over. She seemed able to cope with it during the day and even got to the place where she could objectively examine a specimen without coming completely unglued, but at night it was another story!

Each evening she would sleep for one or two hours and then the nightmares would begin. I'd rush into her room to find her sitting or kneeling in bed frantically brushing thousands of imaginary spiders and ants out of the sheets and blankets. Putting the light on and showing her the empty bed was some comfort, but fear had so emotionally exhausted her that returning to sleep was almost impossible.

Week after week her screaming woke the entire family, and all of us began suffering fatigue from those disastrous nightmares.

I seemed to be able to help Laurie cope with her daytime conscious fears but I hadn't the faintest idea as to how to handle the subconscious ones at night.

Finally, after six weeks of interrupted rest, she screamed out in the night and I ran to her room for the umpteenth time. I was determined to help her give the Lord these fears and then fill up the vacancy that was left. I did not turn on her bedroom light. I simply grabbed her by the shoulders and in one or two movements pulled her down into bed, brought the covers up around her shoulders properly and out loud—in a strong, rather commanding voice, prayed by faith, "Dear Lord, You know Laurie keeps dreaming about spiders. Please take these spider dreams away from her right now and give her good dreams instead. Thank you, Lord, for the good dream she is going to have. Amen."

With that I tucked the blanket under her chin, kissed the little freckle on her nose, and went to bed.

I was putting bread into the toaster the next morning when a cheery voice behind me said, "Guess what!" When I turned, there Laurie stood all smiles, and she said, "I had the best dream *ever!* I dreamed you gave me 25¢, and you said, 'Go into that candy store and buy whatever you want.'"

About a month later, I realized I'd been sleeping the whole night through. "Laurie," I asked, "Are you having any more spider nightmares?"

"Nope," she answered.

"Did they all go away, completely?" I questioned.

"Not all at once," she said. "A couple of nights after you prayed for me, I woke up from a spider dream. I was going to call you but instead I just prayed, 'Dear Lord, take this dream away and give me the good kind,' and He did, so I didn't wake you."

The faith that God could take care of a real fear (even a subconscious one) made our Laurie a shining, sparkling little girl that morning. I'll never forget how beautiful and how rested and relaxed she looked. It really showed!

My mother was beautiful by faith too, and she continually replaced fear by faith. When one of women's greatest fears, the fear of cancer, became a reality in her life, she seized the experience and her faith grew to enormous proportions.

After the removal of one breast, she was having cobalt treatments at U.C.L.A. Medical Center when lumps were discovered in the other breast. Because of a number of factors, including the size of the new tumors, a second mastectomy was ruled out.

Mother was a favorite with doctors, nurses, and attendants alike. A doctor, the chief of staff, told a large gathering of visiting doctors from all over the world about my mother. He stressed in his lecture that when a cancer patient had faith like Mrs. Miller, he was prepared to see anything happen. It could be a brief, temporary remission of the disease or even a dramatic, miraculous recovery. "The key," he said, "is the patient's faith in God." He went on to warn, "If a patient has no faith at all, the course of events is pretty predictable. The patient is dead already."

My mother and I talked much about faith and fear, and one day after a cobalt treatment at the hospital, she excitedly told me what had just happened.

She had been placed on a gurney, one of those narrow beds with wheels, and rolled into a hallway to await her treatments. The nurses all knew of Mother's extraordinary faith, so they often deliberately parked her bed near any patient who was despondent or upset. That day had been no exception, and the patient beside her was sobbing as if her heart would break.

Mother reached across the little space between them and said gently, "What's the matter? What's wrong?"

The woman turned her head and faced Mother with a disgusted, "Are you kidding?" look. "What do you mean, what's wrong? Look where I am. I've got cancer!" she said.

"So do I," said Mother.

"Yes," continued the woman, "but I had surgery for the removal of one breast, and now I've got lumps on the other side."

"So have I," came the quiet response.

"But that's not all," she countered. "These treatments make me violently ill."

"I know, me too," my mother said.

"Besides all that, I'm in my 50s and I think I'm going to die!" Now, the woman was almost shouting.

"I think I am too," came Mother's reflective answer.

At this point, the woman rose up on one elbow to get a better look at my mother and her words hissed and sizzled, "Well, then, how can you lie there so ★@!* peaceful?!"

My mother said she wasn't shocked at the woman's profanity because she well understood the stark fear that propelled and prompted it. She didn't give her a lecture on the sin of using God's name in vain. She simply jumped in with both feet to the heart of the basic problem. "Have you tried praying?"

The woman settled back down, heaved a frustrated sigh and said, "Of course I've prayed! I've gone to every church in our area. I've prayed everything from Christian Scientist to Buddhist and Baptist prayers and you know what? None of them worked."

"I know why," my mother said.

She was back up on her elbow, really listening with, "You *do*? Why?"

"You didn't pray with faith. You've got a terrible need in your life. Someone told you to go see the King and petition Him to help you. So without preparation or invitation, you barged into the King's throne room. You yelled, 'OK, King, I've got cancer, and You had better do something about it. You gave it to me, so You'd better take it back!' Then, because you were so sure He wouldn't help you, you stormed out of His palace without even waiting for a reply. You told your friends and relatives, 'See, I told you so! I went to the King, and He didn't hear me or help me!'

"How different it would have been had you humbly gone before the King of all kings, Jesus, poured out your heart, confessed your sins, and then presented by faith your unbearable needs, in faith asking Him to go with you through this valley, in faith confessing your

need for strength to bear this cancer, and in faith believing that He would *never* leave or forsake you."

The woman's belligerence began to wash away with
the tears that were streaming down her face.

Mother ended with, "You think your essential problem is to get rid of cancer, but what you really need is
Jesus."

All the woman said was, "Pray for me, please—*now.*"

This story was related to me once more, several
weeks after my mother's death, by the head nurse. She
gave me a postscript about the woman. The nurse
said, "We saw a fantastic change in that patient after
your mother prayed for her. She was never depressed
again. In fact, she was like a new woman."

My mother was one of those exceptionally beautiful
women who dared to pray daily the prayer of faith.
Her faith became stronger and more real with time because of the results she saw.

I can't remember the name of the story, but according to a *Reader's Digest* article I once read, no scientist has ever seen an atom. Yet every scientist believes
in atoms because he sees and ascertains the results of
atomic energy.

My mother was not the only one who saw results.
We all saw the consequences of her faith at work, and
it was deeply reflected in her face. She had a unique
beauty in that very often people could not recall a single detail of her face but they would say, "She was the
most beautiful woman I've ever seen."

Peter tells women to be beautiful on the inside because that's a lasting thing and very precious to God.
He says, "That kind of deep beauty was seen in the
saintly women of old, who trusted God and fitted in
with their husbands' plans" (1 Peter 3:5).

My mother's "deep beauty" went hand in hand with
her faith and her unfailing trust in Jesus, her dearest
friend.

By faith you, too, can look at Jesus. You can, by
faith, see that He came,

"To bind up the broken hearted,
  To proclaim liberty to the captives . . .
To comfort all that mourn . . .
To give unto them
    Beauty for ashes,
    The oil of joy for mourning,
    The garment of praise for the spirit of heaviness"
                   (Isa. 61:1-3, KJV).

What an exchange! Think of it! Coming to Christ just as we are and having Him give us beauty for our ashes.

Edna St. Vincent Millay wrote:

"Man then has not invented God;
  He has developed faith,
  To meet a God already there!"*

We have just spent considerable time looking together into God's spiritual mirror. We are aware, or should be, that any deep or lasting beauty inside us is based on the absence of perpetual fears and on a never-ending growth of faith.

But let's look now at the glass mirror above our dresser or sink and see what we have going for us on the outside. What do you see? What do other people see when they look at you? What inner beauty, if any, does your face reflect? What's your best facial feature? What's your hair like? Do you wear makeup, or, if you don't, should you start? These thoughts and many others will probably arise as you look into your reflection.

As I was writing this chapter, my mailman brought a letter from a 23-year-old wife and mother. She had read my book, *His Stubborn Love* and was writing to thank me for it, but she was also troubled about some things in her life. She asked several questions. One was, "I want to be Christ-centered, but I still find myself interested in how I look and how my hair looks. Is it wrong for a Christian to want to look nice?"

*From *Conversations at Midnight*, Harper & Brothers, New York.

The answer is absolutely no; there is nothing wrong with a Christian wanting to look nice! When we have received inward beauty for the ashes of our life, it is bound to show on our faces.

Our faith certainly determines the depth of our facial beauty, but we can definitely help or hinder those outward looks. We can ignore them completely or smother them with all kinds of frills, both of which are wrong.

Your look into the mirror might reveal that you're basically doing what's right for you. Only a tiny push in the right direction may update your hair style, soften a look that has changed with your age, or put to use a new product that's suited to your facial bone structure or coloring. So, keep at it. Don't be afraid to try a new thing or experiment a bit to make the most of your natural looks.

But what if the mirror confirms the suspicion that a lot or everything is wrong? Skin, hair, and figure all seem to need help? We are very fortunate to live in an age when there are many avenues open to us. The training schools, books, or courses, and the prices of each, differ according to your needs and budget.

The most thorough courses in charm and self-improvement are taught at modeling schools.

Pat French, the beauty expert I mentioned before, says that this type of intensive course is excellent for many women because a professional expert can take a personalized interest in you. She can give you the specific help you need. She's well qualified to help organize your grooming habits. She may be the first person to help you realize your good traits and minimize your flaws—especially the ones you have no control over like big feet, a narrow face, or 6'2" height.

When Pat was a teen-ager and a student at modeling school herself, she had a teacher whom she credits with being used by the Lord in her life.

"This modeling teacher," Pat said, "was of enormous help to me. She was aware of what was wrong with my looks and immediately started to help me compensate. She also looked for good traits, and I learned I had certain little talents and beauty traits which had escaped all notice of relatives, friends, and previous teachers. Nobody else had seen those traits!"

I'm sure nobody misses those beauty traits today in Pat because she is a beautiful blonde (or dazzling red-head, depending on which wig she is wearing), and the overall picture is marvelous.

If you don't need quite this specialized type of course, there are other opportunities. Some churches, like ours, have marvelous courses for women. The girls that come out of that class at our church are glowingly feminine. Then there are a number of health spas and gyms to restore or reshape your figure. Even in department stores, you can find help. Semiprofessional cosmetic sales girls can give you a quick facial survey and help you toward balanced beauty.

To stimulate your thinking, here is a list of some basic ABC's required for outward beauty.

1. *Clean, clean skin*

Basic to all beauty is head-to-toe cleanliness, but it's particularly important with regard to your face. Use cold or warm creams, lotions—anything to get it clean. Some beauty experts feel soap dries the natural oils and accelerates the aging process, so go easy on soap. Find the one that works for you and use it! After a good cleaning, you might want to finish off with an astringent. It closes the pores. By the way, keep all beauty supplies (like brushes) clean too.

2. *Sensible makeup foundation*

Few of us have the flawless, unblemished, peaches-and-cream skin I saw yesterday on an 18-year-old beauty. Most likely we have red skin blotches, lines, bone structure irregularities, and, at least once a month, a delicately shaped circle of blue under our eyes.

I personally use Merle Norman's foundation base as it covers without looking like a thick layer of paint, and it *suits* me. Our daughter has super-sensitive, allergic-to-anything skin, and she uses Almay cosmetics.

Whatever you choose, a liquid or a cream, in a tube or a jar, a stick or a cake, the main point is to cover blemishes with something that will not turn orange or chalky-white, cause a rash or look like it's an inch thick. Remember too, every face needs some kind of moisturizer, just as a garden needs rain.

3. *Sparkling eyes*

Since our eyes are the "windows of our souls," everyone from Aunt Mabel in Podunk to Mollie the fashion model in Paris should give attention to the care and beauty of the eyes. If there are very few women who can go without foundation makeup, there are even fewer who can go eye-less into the world.

However, if you are 17 years old and have large, stunning, blue eyes with long, thick, softly curled black eyelashes, you can skip this part. You don't need any help. For the rest, discover your eyes by starting at the top and working down.

A. Pluck out stray hairs, and thin your eyebrows where it's necessary. You may need to use an eyebrow pencil or brush to fill in some sparse spots, but remember that the harder you lay on that pencil, the harder the look becomes.

B. There are all colors and kinds of eye shadow. Use it sparingly in the daylight hours but enjoy it for evening. It will add a soft, glowing sparkle to your eyes, and it will usually pick up extra colors that are hidden in the iris of the eye. Your general eye color may be brown or blue, but if you look at your eyes in a magnifying mirror you'll see all kinds of colors. That's why, when you wear a dress of a certain shade or hue, your eyes seem to change color. Anyway, experiment with colors in eye shadows. Use it sparingly, however, because you're not dressing up to be in a circus.

C. Invest that dollar or two for an eyelash curler. Just as curls around or by your face soften it, so does curling the eyelashes. The look is feathery and pretty. Then use mascara to thicken and darken.

D. Perhaps you don't have eyelashes long enough to get a curler around. By all means, try wearing false eyelashes. Before you pounce on me for *such* a suggestion, I don't mean you should look like the girl who wears false eyelashes so long one must stand three feet away to avoid getting swept up in their backlash. I'm not suggesting the extreme look in lashes. As a matter of fact, most false lashes need trimming and sizing to fit the individual's eyelid. You might need only the small addition of a demi-lash to give a fuller look. Remember, in order to enhance our looks, we women of today wear a number of false items; wigs, dentures, and padded bras, to name a few. So, take a good front and side view look in the mirror and see if you can enhance the windows of your soul.

4. *Lips:* to color or not to color?

Ah, here was the great sin of the 1920s and '30s— especially if the lipstick was really out-and-out red. Color in the 1940s went to a deep purple-red. In the 1950s, it dissolved into clear reds, but by the middle 60s, it dwindled down to soft pinks and light oranges. In the late 1960s some regressed to a pure death-like white. Teen-agers looked ghoulish, and older women looked as if they had been dead for days. At the beginning of the 1970s, pale pinks were back—made with new textures. "Frosted and creamy" or "polished and wet" became the look of lipsticks. Since fads tend to repeat themselves every 20 years, I predict that by the end of the 70s we'll be back to dark purple-reds again.

What should *you* wear? Find the shade that softens or flatters your face, and use it in good taste. You need a lipstick that's light and sheer, yet covers completely. This same advice goes for coloring your cheeks with blush—softness is the rule. The older you get, the more pastel you should go.

One other word on lipstick—*never* apply it or any makeup in a public place. After a meal in a restaurant, church banquet hall, or private home, go to a rest room to restore worn off makeup, and mend your fences alone! Truly ugly is the woman who gets out her little mirror and crudely goes through all her personal restoration acts in front of everybody.

5. *Alive hair*

The Bible says the very hairs of our head are numbered. If our hair is that important to the Lord, then surely there are a number of things we should do in caring for and maintaining our hair.

We must keep it clean. Use a quality shampoo and a conditioning rinse. Don't skimp on either item. You could end up with permanently damaged hair.

Seek out a hairdresser or even a good men's barber for a haircut, trim, or style change as often as needed. If it's been two years since you had someone change or really work on your hair, you are past due! Make an appointment tomorrow. If you can't afford professional services, ask around; you may find someone who knows a talented teen ager who is a whiz with the scissors or home permanent kits.

This mini-beauty course of ABC requirements for enhancing outward beauty is very basic, but it might mean the difference between confirming and denying the faith that is within you.

It would be wonderful if we could stand at a distance and see ourselves as God and men see us. Maybe we would immediately be able to properly evaluate our looks. But all we really have is God's mirror (His Word) for our faith and our dressing room mirror for our face. Let's use them both enthusiastically to be the beautiful women of faith and face God intended.

Additional verses:

1 Peter 1:21
Proverbs 22:17-19

Faith working in us: Psalm 4:8
Psalm 32:8

Trust: Psalm 55:17
                                    Psalm 46:1-3
                                    Psalm 94:19
                                    Psalm 91:5

Beauty: 2 Corinthians 3:18

CHAPTER FOUR

WORRY: A SCAMPERING MOUSE

The world is full of worry,
Everlasting worry;
Worry about this and worry about that,
Worry a little and worry a lot,
Worry with nothing to worry about,
Just worry, worry, worry.
                 C. T. Weigle

A tense, fidgety, overwrought young woman I'll call Ivy did not sit across from me on my couch—she nervously perched. Her shoulders never touched the back cushions, and she moved restlessly along the outer edges of the couch as she talked.

Worry is a mouse,
A small scampering thing
With sharp tiny feet,
That scurries over our soul.

Quite visibly, the mouse of worry not only was scampering over Ivy's soul, but over her face, her hands, and her body motions, as well. All the "worries" in her life created a jumpy, highly disturbed young woman.

She talked on and on non-stop. Often she interrupted herself to digress from one subject to another. Her comments were defensive, often critical, and occasionally filled with self-pity. Once in a while, her speech was punctuated by a nervous, high-pitched laugh, which was accompanied by some weird facial expression. Her restless hands tugged at her skirt, then nervously twisted a strand of hair. Her slender fingers ended in ugly stumps of bitten-off nails. The once pretty face was a distorted, ugly mess of conflicts and inner anguish.

The effects and consequences of worry were evident in every area of Ivy's being.

Let me list some of those consequences, for I see them in any woman who is a habitual worrier.

1. *Worry borrows*

It's a disease of the future. It borrows the unknown trouble of tomorrow. The worrier loses the beautiful spirit of hope because worry paints such a gloomy, shocking, dreadful picture of the future. She becomes deeply troubled about something that very well may never take place, or she worries about something that happened 30 years ago that can't possibly be changed now.

2. *Worry broods*

It simmers on some back burner in the depths of a woman's mind. It limits activity and curtails creativity. It is like a brood hen sitting on the nest of her mind. (If she broods long enough, she will hatch a flock of troubles—real or imagined.)

3. *Worry is a mental burden*

Seneca, many centuries ago, said, "The mind that is anxious about the future is miserable." A woman's worry affects her mental ability to act wisely and severely limits her mental power to think logically and clearly. Her mind locks into a standard position: *miserable*. I wonder what David was worried about when he wrote, "My mind is filled with apprehension and with gloom" (Ps. 6:3).

This state of mind might not be too terrible if it affected only the woman, but it is highly contagious! Soon others catch it, and the woman finds she has infected her family, business associates, and friends as well. She wonders why she has a hard time keeping a friend. She also wonders why so few people ever *really* ask, "How are you?"

4. *Worry is a physical burden*

There seems to be little doubt that worry *kills*. It may not be as swift as cancer, but it is just as deadly. Worry acts like

> a poison in the blood,
> a drain on inner vitality,
> a stiffening in the joints,
> a hardening of the arteries,

and very often it is the cause of an ulcer.

A woman can experience real pain from mental worries. Ralph Waldo Emerson once spoke of ". . . the torments of pain you endured, from evils that never arrived."

5. *Worry robs*

It steals the magic sparkle from a woman's eyes. It takes the alive, alert quality from her appearance and substitutes dullness in its place. Worry confiscates a woman's ability to smile and permanently etches a frown into the lines of her face, adding years to her looks.

6. *Worry is a habit*

Life is full of habits—good and bad—but a worrying woman is often so close to her habit that she does not see it for the bad one it is. The habit of worry holds a death-like grip on her whole life.

7. *Worry is absolutely useless*

It never helps any situation. It blinds a woman to possible solutions and makes her real problems tougher and more complicated. It always clouds or muddies up the issues involved.

In *Letters To His Son*, Lord Chesterfield said, "I recommend you to take care of the minutes, for the hours will take care of themselves." But the worrying woman is too bound, worrying about her problems, to take care of either the minutes or the hours.

8. Worry is definitely a sin

While worry is a natural, human emotion we all experience, it becomes definitely a sin when we let it take over our thoughts. It clearly reveals a woman's lack of faith in God's ability to work out the details of her life. It reflects a verdict against God's faithfulness, and it brings reproach on His name, because it means the worrier really doesn't think God sufficient for her problem.

Once, when I was talking with my mother about this very thing—the sin of worrying—she said, "You're right, worry is a sin for the Christian woman. But the unsaved, the non-Christian . . . ah, there's a different story. She has a right, almost a duty, to worry, because she has no Christ to rely on as we do!"

The young woman who twisted and turned on my couch that day typified many women I've seen over the past few years. I'm no stranger to the worry written all over her because I've seen it in my own life and in my own family.

Ever since I can remember, I have loved my identical twin aunts: Aunt Harriet and Aunt Hortense. I've learned one lesson after another from these two darlings. They are well into their 70s now, but they have always been beautiful women. Even as young girls, they won one of the first national toothpaste "smile" contests! They were not only identical in looks but shared identical tastes and preferences.

One would go to town, purchase some article, perhaps clothing or shoes, and come home to find the other had bought the same article (from the same store and the same salesman).

Both aunts married and lived most of their lives in the same town and neighborhood, separated by only a few blocks. A few years ago they both became widows.

Over the years, something has happened to their "identical" look. It's hard to explain because they still look alike physically, yet the "inner" essence of fragrance in one is different from the other. One looks older (and not by 20 minutes, either!), more depressed, strained, and tense. The other has an alive, alert quality that instantly draws you to her.

Once we (as a family) accepted the twins as they were, with their very opposite personalities, they became a delightful study in contrasts and still are.

When we first meet, I continue to have trouble telling them apart for a minute or so, and then I'll take a closer look or one will say something and the matter of identity is quickly settled.

After I moved to California from Michigan, they wrote me priceless letters. Their letters always arrived within two or three days of each other and both covered the same subjects. However, there was an amazing difference in their attitudes. I have prepared composite letters which typify their correspondence through the years. Can you detect the worried tone of Aunt Harriet's?

Dear Joyce,

We are having a terrible snowstorm. It's going to go into a blizzard. No lettuce this spring, and the farmers say this weather is to blame.

Your Uncle Walter couldn't drive to work today, so he had to walk all that way. He can't stand too much of that cold wind and those icy streets.

Mrs. Brondage, down the street, slipped just last week and fractured her hip. Not two days before, I *told* her that would happen.

I'm not feeling good at all, so I can't get out to prayer meeting. Even when I do go, I don't see too many there. Seems like people aren't interested in spiritual things any more. I've quit teaching my Sunday School class. Those little children make me too nervous for words.

Uncle Greg flew to Chicago yesterday. I hope he doesn't crash. You can't trust those airplanes. Just read the newspaper—airplanes crash all the time.

Well, I've got to close as I want to hear the 6 o'clock news. My, things are in terrible shape all over the world. I wonder how long all of this can go on. It's awful.

Love,
Aunt Harriet

Soon after I read her letter, Aunt Hortense's cheery epistle would arrive—and what a contrast.

Dearest Joyce,

You should see the beautiful snow! It's been coming down for hours and everything is white and sparkly. We've had a pretty cold winter so far, but you know that makes great apples and cherries later on!

Cars aren't doing too well on the streets so your Uncle Walter had to walk to work. I think that's great. He needs the fresh air and exercise.

Mrs. Brondage, our neighbor, slipped and fell last week. Today I took her some homemade soup. She seemed pleased, and much better.

I haven't been too well this year, but I'm able to get out to prayer meeting once in a while. There are not too many out but the Lord said, "Where two or three are gathered, there am I in the midst," so the Lord comes on Wednesday, even when we don't. I'm still teaching my Sunday School class after all these years. My, how I love those dear little tykes.

Your Uncle Greg flew to Chicago yesterday. Isn't that something?! Just think, from here to there in a few minutes—what a wonder.

Must close, I want to catch the news. My, when you hear all that's going on in the world today—wars, murders, and what have you—aren't you glad you know Jesus? And that He is in control and cares for us? I am!

Love,
Aunt Hortense

All their letters have been like vivid maps. In great

detail they show exactly how and where the twins live out their lives.

A few summers ago I was back East on a speaking engagement and, to my joy, the relatives decided to have a family reunion picnic. The twin aunts were the last to arrive. I saw them get out of a car, so I ran across the park to greet them. As I got closer, it dawned on me how much they still looked alike. I laughed because I couldn't tell them apart. When I reached them, I hugged the first one I came to, and said, "Whom do I have here?"

My aunt gave me a great big smile and playfully refused to tell me her name. Out of the corner of my eye I saw the sober look on the other twin's face and heard her sum up the whole thing rather well with, "I'm the other one."

Instantly, I knew I was holding and hugging Aunt Hortense. Her optimistic, God-will-take-care-of-everything spirit has kept her warm and vibrant.

That day in the park, I loved watching both of them. The children of my cousins swarmed over Aunt Hortense like bees finding a field of blossoms. Aunt Harriet—worn down by years of worry—cooly remarked, "I don't know how she stands those noisy children climbing all over her!"

The woman who worries misses all the sunshine of life because she's forever expecting rain. She makes a storm out of a shower, a disaster out of a disappointment. She looks for the day to bring failures and losses and, when it does, she's the first to say, "I told you so!"

No one is immune to worrisome circumstances or problems. Difficult situations confront all of us in one way or another. Sometimes they come upon us with surprising suddenness. This surprise is a kind of numbing, shock experience; and, actually, it can help us at the time. It's nature's way of carrying us through the hardest moment of grief or crisis.

Perhaps you've experienced this: you've been driving on the freeway and have watched an accident happen all around you. You surprise yourself by managing to drive calmly, bravely, even skillfully through it without a scratch. Then, when you're completely safe, you've pulled over to an off ramp and gone completely to pieces.

We seem to survive the worse moments in life with a superior kind of instinctive courage. But afterwards —what then? When the surprise and the numbness pass, worry begins, and we fall apart.

Let me emphasize that it *is* natural to worry. Yet, it is not in God's plan for us to spend our every waking moment worrying over each detail of our lives.

The world in which we live is full of very large problems. Each day brings new issues that must be dealt with. Not one of these issues, big or small, can be solved by the loss of sleep, by tied-up nerves, by headaches, backaches, or by any other companions of worry.

The woman who honestly wants to sweep the mouse of worry out of her soul has got to start right there: with her soul. What is her personal relationship to Jesus? The biggest obstacle to inner beauty in the world today is the sin problem.

Go back for a moment to Ivy, the young woman on my couch. The basic issue of her relationship with Jesus was where I began when she had finished baring her soul. It was a joyous moment that day when we prayed together and she gave Christ her life. She took the leap over the sin obstacle and was off and running toward God's beauty.

Ivy has never been the same since the basic issue of sin was settled and she was forgiven by God. She's taken a 180 degree turn from tensely anticipating everything to taking life as it comes, with God's peace. But worry is a habit. To overcome it, she brings the first worry of the morning (and all the little ones that follow) to the Saviour's attention. She knows that now, since she is God's child, habitual worry is a sin for her. She knows, too, that sin is the only thing that separates her from God's loving care.

David knew how important it is to have God's daily

forgiveness for sin. He wrote, "I know You get no pleasure from wickedness and cannot tolerate the slightest sin." (Ps. 5:4).

Worry is one of those "slightest sins," but the worry habit can be deeply ingrained.

When Ivy became a Christian, she did not drop her worry automatically. She had her worry habit years before she accepted Christ, and it would have continued had she not recognized the issues involved. I'm happy to report that Ivy is bringing her worry problems to Jesus, with astonishing results.

A bad habit must be broken and banished in order for faith to have a place to grow. Any habit can be broken—from alcoholism to fingernail biting to a nervous giggle—*if* the possessor of the habit has a real desire to put a stop to it and *if* something constructive is put in its place.

Previously I stated that worry is a mental burden. Ivy has taken her mind (the one that would continue to worry) and has begun to use it constructively. She looks at Proverbs 20:24, and it makes great sense to her. "Since the Lord is directing our steps, why try to understand everything that happens along the way?" The logic of this verse relieves some mental pressure, and almost instantly you can see Ivy relax in God's peace. She has, in just a few weeks, been transformed from a caterpillar into a gorgeous butterfly.

Now, see if you can follow this:

If we believe that God's power can give a man or a woman brains—then we can believe that God's power can govern the brain He made.

If God's power can govern the brain, then it can keep that brain organized, neat, and orderly.

If God's power can make an orderly brain, then it can put worry into the inconspicuous and unimportant corner of our mind where worry belongs. It's like sweeping the kitchen floor until all the dust is in one corner.

If God's power can localize the worry, relegating

it to a small heap, then it can also furnish the dustpan that will take worry off the floor of our brain entirely and provide the ash heap on which to toss it! We can enjoy our spic-and-span mind because of God's mighty power at work.

The instant the mouse of worry tries to sneak in, use your mind to believe God completely! Admit Him into your life completely! Admit the width of His resources, the height of His intellect, and the depth of His love.

Why do you suppose Paul told us so precisely what to think on in his letter to the Philippians? I'm sure he knew about the times we tend to think worrisome thoughts. He knew too, that we become whatever we think about. So he wrote down a great mental health principle to think and live by.

He knew if we would concentrate our thinking on

> truth,
> goodness,
> pure and lovely things,
> fine and good traits in others,
> praise and gratefulness to God,

we'd have very little time for the negative, destructive thinking which worry produces. Also, we'd become like our thoughts (cf. Phil 4:8).

An unknown writer penned the following prayer, and if your life is tied up in knots with the sin of worry, read it carefully. Perhaps as you slowly read it, you can breathe in God's calming beauty; then, exhale the restless tension of your life. If you will ask God to meet your need and break your habit, He will. He'll replace fretful worries with His very own restful peace.

Slow me down, Lord! Ease the pounding of my heart by the quieting of my mind. Steady my hurried pace with a vision of the eternal reach of times. Give me, amidst the confusion of my day, the calmness of the everlasting hills. Break the tension of my nerves and muscles with the soothing music of the singing streams that live in my memory. Help me to know the magical restorative power of sleep. Teach me the art of taking minute vacations . . . of slowing down to look at a flower, to chat with a friend, to pat a dog, to read a few lines from a good book.

Remind me each day of the fable of the hare and the tortoise that I may know that the race is not always to the swift; that there is more to life than increasing its speed. Let me look upward into the branches of the towering oak, and know that it grew because it grew slowly and well. Slow me down, Lord, and inspire me to send my roots deep into the soil of life's enduring values, that I may grow toward the stars of your rewards. Amen.

Additional Verses:

The promises *of God*	Psalm 27:14 Psalm 34:15-20 Psalm 37:3-7 2 Corinthians 7:5,6 Colossians 2:6
Our minds	Psalm 51:10 Proverbs 12:5 1 Corinthians 2:16b 1 Corinthians 3:20 Romans 12:2

CHAPTER FIVE

THE CALMING BEAUTY
OF PRAYER

One Saturday morning my husband and I were discussing over a leisurely breakfast, how very much we are looking forward to being grandparents. We discovered that we shared a common eagerness for our children to present us with grandchildren. In the midst of our talk, we had to laugh because neither Laurie (age 17) or Rick (age 19) are even married, much less giving us grandchildren. Yet, there we sat, lovingly imagining how dear it would be to be grandparents.

As I've reflected on that morning, I've realized the desire to be a grandmother was instilled in me by my mother who was something else as a grandma to our children.

Grandma had everything going for her all the time. She'd arrive at our house with a bag of "stuff." Sometimes it was a fun T-shirt for Rick or a playsuit for Laurie. Other times it was one stick of gum. "Saved, just for *you*," Grandma would lovingly explain.

But the relationship I loved observing the most was the way my mother created a secret, a surprise, or an adventure with our children.

Mother always talked to me, but she whispered to our children. They had all sorts of highly personal conversations. The children included everything from how they got that big scratch on their leg to what great thing they'd seen in the park that day. All was confidentially shared.

She taught them a thousand things in her short time with them, but I'm most grateful for her thorough but brief lessons on prayer. She made praying as easy as breathing for our children, even though Laurie was a preschooler at the time. "No fuss, no muss, just talk to the Lord about it," was her attitude.

After she died, I found her personal definition of prayer in one of her notebooks. It read,

Personal prayer, it seems to me, is a simple necessity of life. It's as basic to an individual as sunshine, food, and water—and at times, of course, much more so!

Personal prayer, I believe, is our effort to get in touch with the infinite God. Oh, I know my prayers are imperfect. Of course they are, but then I'm an imperfect human being. (But God knows *that* already.)

A thousand experiences have convinced me, beyond a shadow of a doubt, that prayer multiplies the strength of an individual and brings within the scope of his capabilities almost any conceivable objective!

Time and time again, I'd see Laurie or Rick up on Grandma's lap and hear them pouring out some trouble to her. If I strained my ears, I'd usually hear Mother responding by praying something like, "Now, Jesus, You know all about Billy down the street, and You know how he throws rocks. Please help Billy to stop doing that, and help Laurie to show Billy how to play and have fun. Amen." Then she'd add some words about, "Maybe Billy doesn't like his house, or his red hair or something. Maybe he needs love." Grandmother and child would spend time together discussing the seriousness of the situation, and Jesus was always in on everything.

After she had these sessions with our children, I would be utterly stunned at the calming beauty of her prayers with them.

The woman, the teen-ager, or the child that can slip

easily into prayer has a beauty formula going for her that no cosmetic on the market can beat.

It seems strange to me that in spite of all the great books we read on prayer, we still miss its exciting importance in our lives.

Prayer is a fascinating spiritual voyage of discovery. Explorers in the realm of prayer are a little like Columbus when he landed on a new continent.

In blind faith he had begged support for his adventure, sailed unknown seas, and found a new land without having any idea as to what opportunities lay beyond.

We probably have only just reached the edge of the beach in prayer. A vast, unknown continent lies beyond us, waiting to be explored, conquered, and cultivated. Nothing can be so thrilling as discovery, but some of us are so comfortable in our prayer rut that the mere thought of exploring tires us out completely.

Beautiful is the woman who joins in the highest of all discovery by adventuring into prayer. Just think, she doesn't need to leave home, work, or career. She doesn't need to stop any task she might be doing to carry on this adventure because she carries God's mind in hers! She is with God every second, and He is with her.

Some women make an issue out of the verse, "Pray without ceasing" (1 Thes. 5:17, KJV).

"How can that possibly be?" they question. "Does that mean we are to stop everything, fold our hands, close our eyes, and stay that way all day?"

Absolutely not! There should be one time during the day when you give God your undivided attention. Then He can speak to you, and you can clearly hear Him. But just as your mind and soul are with you all the time, so is the Lord! Praying is as easy and effortless as breathing. God is here and ahead of us. If we stand still, He stands. If we move, He has already moved ahead, and we begin to know the joy of walking in His direction.

Over and over again, I've been asked if God really speaks to me, and if He does, how does He do it? It's not such a big mystery. Haven't you been grocery shopping or ironing and had a thought about a friend fly through your mind? It's someone you haven't thought of in months, so you get to wondering how they are. Next, the thought that you should call, write, or go see them whizzes across your thinking. So, you stop what you are doing and call them. After your hello, you may hear, "Oh, I've been hoping you'd call; I really need you. I'm so grateful you called!"

My minister friend, Keith, has told me of many incidents of driving along the street and the thought (definitely from the Lord) would occur that he should turn at the next street and visit the Smiths or the Browns who live there. He's turned up the street, stopped at the house, rung the doorbell, and quietly listened as Mrs. Smith or Mrs. Brown says, "Oh, thank God, you've come! Please come in. We need you. We were just talking about you and we were wishing you were here."

Another friend, Bo Knowlton, told me she was sewing up the seams in her new drapes when the name of her oldest son "popped" into her mind. Since she had a fearful feeling about him, she stopped sewing and breathed, "Lord, I know Dan is in Your hands, but I don't understand these terrible feelings. Please take care of him; he's Yours."

She went back to sewing; yet she continued mentally to hold Dan before the Lord. The bad vibrations grew stronger all afternoon, so she called a friend and, while admitting that everything was probably just fine with Dan, they still prayed and especially asked the Lord to keep him safe.

Much later, when Dan was supposed to be home for dinner, she got a phone call from him. He was in a hospital and had been slightly hurt. All the players of his basketball team were on their way to a game in a neighboring city when the bus had gone off the road on a sharp curve, and only by a miracle had it come to a stop just on the edge of a high precipice. There were no serious injuries, and Dan was just checking with Mom to tell her he was all right.

God speaks to us by the Holy Spirit's gentle voice in our minds. If that Spirit is unhindered, the voice of God can be remarkably clear.

If you haven't heard the Lord speaking directly to you, the key might lie in examining what in your life may have silenced the Holy Spirit.

There are a number of hindrances in our prayer lives that bring what could be an adventurous experience down to an apathetic journey into boredom. Let me list three of the most common hindrances:

1. *You have not opened your life completely to Christ.*

You may be like the woman in the hospital with my mother who had prayed many prayers but all without faith, without Jesus, and without God's forgiveness. You must be born again and become as a child before you have access to God the Father.

Speaking to God is a little like speaking to the president of the United States. Because I have seen many pictures of our president, I would know him if I saw him in person. Because I have heard him over the air, I would recognize his voice if he spoke to me. If he ever invited me to dinner in the White House, I'd be able to say, "I've talked with the president." I'd know his thinking on some matters and his wishes and desires concerning certain issues and policies.

But there is no way that I could have access to him, his thinking, or his help, as do his daughters! They are privileged. They have immediate access. They have priority. They are loved. They talk freely with the president, who is their father.

We have to be God's children. It is not enough to know what God is like, or in an emergency to "hear" His voice or use His Word like a rabbit's foot for luck.

And the only way to become God's child, to be born into His family, is to receive Jesus Christ as personal Saviour. "But as many as received Him, to them gave

He power to become the sons of God, even to them that believe on His name" (John 1:12, KJV).

2. *You are harboring a long-time bitterness or daily committing sin.*

It doesn't seem to matter how small or how big one's bitterness or sin is but rather that it is there. You may cherish a small resentment against your parents because they never took you to a dentist to have your teeth straightened. You may be bitter over a mother who, early in life, convinced you that you were artless and totally uncreative. Your father might have been an absentee father who always had time for business associates (or people in his congregation, as ministers are prone to do) but never shared any of himself with you.

You might be bitter because of a loved one's death or your own debilitating lingering illness. Whatever its cause, bitterness will hopelessly clog the prayer channels to God. Known sin also separates one from God, and even though you may be a Christian, the Lord will not hear your prayers.

John 15:7 says, "But if you stay in Me and obey My commands, you may ask any request you like, and it will be granted!"

3. *You aren't specific in your prayers.*

James knew about this lack of specifics when he wrote, "Ye have not because ye ask not" (James 4:2, KJV). Besides that, it's easier to be concerned for the "whole world of lost pagans" than the man we work for or the woman who checks our groceries at the store. When we generalize our prayers, it takes out the risk of our direct involvement. We don't have to chance an adverse reaction from distant heathen, but we do take risks when we relate to a neighbor. It costs nothing to love the nameless lost, but it costs everything to love the individuals we live with and know.

These are only a few of the reasons you may not have prayer's quiet, calming beauty evident in your life.

The woman who has truly asked Christ to come into

her life can have a wise, sane, yet wildly exciting prayer life. Here are some suggestions to help you achieve a beautiful prayer time.

1. *Examine your thoughts.*

Start with a house cleaning of your mental faculties. See what thoughts need to be thrown out of the closets of your mind. The bitter memories, the resentful attitudes toward others, and the grudges you have long harbored need to be banished. It may mean going to someone and asking forgiveness.

James tells us, "Admit your faults to one another and pray for each other so that you may be healed. The earnest prayer of a righteous man has great power and wonderful results" (James 5:16).

Or, in your particular case, it may mean breaking the habit of showing your resentment towards someone by always being critical of them.

Read the entire passage, Colossians 3:12-15, but pay particular attention to the middle part where Paul says, "Be gentle and ready to forgive; never hold grudges. Remember, the Lord forgave you, so you must forgive others."

In Ephesians, Paul talks about "making allowances for each other's faults because of your love" (4:2). So, clean out the grudges and memories and start with a fresh mind.

2. *Be wise in prayer.*

My pastor, Dr. Edward Cole, tells the story of a little girl who was asked what she would pray for if she were stone blind. She thought a moment and then answered, "I'd ask God for a dog with a collar and a chain to lead me around."

We pray a good many prayers like that—asking for a dog and a chain when we could ask for opened eyes. We are foolish in the way we pray repetitious prayers or ask for such petty things.

We can be wise in praying if we remember that prayer is a two-way thing. God is here! He is with us by the power of the Holy Spirit. We have this delightful, hope-filled promise in Romans 8:26, 27: "The Holy

Spirit helps us with our daily problems and in our praying. For we don't even know what we should pray for, nor how to pray as we should; but the Holy Spirit prays for us with such feeling that it cannot be expressed in words. And the Father who knows all hearts knows, of course, what the Spirit is saying as He pleads for us in harmony with God's own will."

See? He made us and He knows us. He has not left us alone to fumble helplessly for words or to grapple feebly after God's miraculous power. The Holy Spirit even prays *for* us. Fantastic!

3. *Make a prayer list.*

Many authorities are suggesting the practical and therapeutic use of lists. Dr. Joyce Brothers has a whole book on making lists.

One of my favorite friends and co-workers is Dr. James Dobson. In his brief but wonderful chapter, "A Moment for Mom," in *Dare to Discipline,**he says:

> When the work load gets particularly heavy, there is comfort to be found in making a list of the duties to be performed. The advantages of writing down one's responsibilities are threefold: (1) You know you aren't going to forget anything. (2) You can guarantee that the most important jobs will get done first. Thus, if you don't get finished by the end of the day, you will have at least done the items that were most critical. (3) The tasks are crossed off the list as they are completed, leaving a record of what has been accomplished.

Almost the identical points can be made in regard to a prayer list. A prayer list:

1. Helps you to be specific and remember all needs.
2. Helps you to see what percentage of your prayers is for physical or material needs, and what percentage is for spiritual needs. It helps you see what the main priorities really are.

*Tyndale House Publishers, Wheaton, Ill., 1970.

3. Helps you keep records so you avoid the rut of habit-prayed prayers. It also keeps track of personal miracles.

Since most of our daily lives seem to move at jet speed—and non-stop—lists are a valuable tool for keeping up with things. Otherwise, what we were desperately praying over two weeks ago may seem nothing compared to today's frantic concerns. In fact, to be truthful, we can't remember exactly what it was two weeks ago that took all our prayer time. But if you've kept a notebook and listed the requests, you can readily see God's hand at work.

My little notebook is the 29¢ variety. I've put the name of the month at the top, written my requests down the left side, and marked off room down the right to fill in answers.

Remember the story of the people who gathered at the church to pray for much needed rain? Only one brought an umbrella. When you make a list of requests, be sure you make room for a list of answers, because according to our faith God will answer.

I gave my husband the first of many spiral notebooks several years ago. Dick keeps it in the car, flips it open each morning, and on the way to work, chats with the Lord about each entry. This month's list reads:

Bank assignment: Northern California?
Joyce's new book.
Laurie dating Don.
Bank audit this month.

I'm sharing this very personal list with you because Dick asked me if I had read his prayer list lately, and when I answered no, he suggested I should, because Laurie had driven his car sometime that week and had written in his book.

She had read the entry, "Laurie dating Don," and had drawn a line down the page to these words:

Dad,

I thank you with my whole heart for praying for Don and me. There are times when I become so frustrated in our relationship. [He is a marvelous young man but has not had a real personal relationship with Christ as Laurie has.] I pray you and Mom will try to continue to understand. You both are terrific parents. You have helped me to know the difference between right and wrong.

I love you, Daddy, and you are always in my prayers.

Love,
Laurie

A few pages later, there was an addition.

Good morning, Dad,

I will be praying for you this morning. Please keep praying for me. My heart is burdened for Don. I never realized how much I could care for and like someone, but the difference of him not being a Christian is so great. I realize that he's in the Lord's hands, but sometimes it's so hard.

I thank God each morning for you. Have a good day at the bank.

I love you, Dad.

Love,
L.J.

"Teach them to obey everything that I have commanded you. I am with you always even unto the end of the world." Amen.

P.S. I hope you don't mind me writing in *"your"* prayer book.

Neither Dick Nor I minded, but as Dick said, "It's awfully hard to read her words and then drive the freeway without tears blurring your vision."

Without this little book in Dick's car, we might have been denied a look into our 17-year-old daughter's heart. How beautifully the Lord helped her share her innermost feelings so we can really "zero in" with prayer over this situation. After all, what better gift do we have to give her than our specific prayers? (Incidentally, Laurie broke up with Don the very next week after writing the last entry in Dick's book. Since he was not a Christian, they just did not have enough in common.)

Cover your own list with your hand after you have prayed over each entry, and then thank God for working each problem out, for giving each answer, and for showing His loving will in each circumstance.

He is the same yesterday, today, and tomorrow, and your list will be just one more proof to encourage you.

4. *Try praying with someone.*

A familiar verse in Matthew states that where two or three are gathered in Christ's name, He is in the midst of them. But the verse just before that always gets to me. Jesus says, "I also tell you this—if two of you agree down here on earth concerning anything you ask for, my Father in Heaven will do it for you" (Matt. 18:19).

At our house we pray individually in our bedrooms and collectively at meal time, but we also pray for each other when one member of the family is leaving for work or school. There is always a quick prayer between my husband and me when he leaves for work. It takes place in the garage with me bent halfway into the car window on the driver's side, and is usually two or three sentences long. It tells God we love Him. It tells Dick I love him. It tells me I'm needed. Daily it demonstrates the truth that prayer will quench the spirit of hate, fear, and panic, when nothing else will even come close.

I have an even quicker prayer with our teen-agers. (They always run a little late.) It's surprising how much I've learned about our children's inner feelings and conflicts by asking them what I should pray about on any given morning. Once, before I could ask, Rick anticipated the question, and said, "Ten o'clock. Zoology class. Test."

Now, at this writing, I'm sure a woman in Pomona High School's attendance office has no idea that one of her helpers (Laurie) prays for her each morning. That's not coming easily for Laurie because she and this woman are not too fond of each other. The other day I asked the Lord to give Laurie the ability to smile when she was working with her. Laurie dryly observed when I had finished, "There you go, Mother, expecting miracles again!"

It was Dr. Ralph Byron, surgeon at City of Hope hospital in Duarte, Calif., who gave Dick and me the greatest clue to praying together. He told me to find the best time for us to pray (morning, night, or whenever) and then suggested the idea of each of us leading on alternate days. One day I'd introduce a sentence prayer on Request No. 1. Then Dick would pray about that subject. Then I'd introduce Request No. 2, and he'd pray, and so on. He prayed short, to-the-point prayers on as many subjects as I wanted to bring up. The next night, Dick would do the introducing. We have been praying this way for over five years, and I can't tell you how close it has brought us to the Lord and to each other.

You may not *have* a husband to pray with. You may have a non-Christian husband, who won't pray with you. You may have a Christian husband who is unwilling to join you in prayer. Don't let any of these hinder you from finding someone with whom to share this exciting prayer discovery. Modify it to suit your life, but by all means *try it*.

You can also pray while you sit in your church. I firmly believe that if every person in a congregation prayed intensely while the pastor preached, we'd see miracle after miracle happen. If your church is dying spiritually, it may not be the fault of the pastor or of the Lord. Maybe the congregation is failing to pray.

The Holy Spirit is ever eager to break through to us,

and He finds an open door where Christians lovingly, joyously unite in prayer.

5. *Discover the joy of praying for someone else.*

When we were little children, our prayers tended to be simple, happy demands on Jesus. Children ask for small favors like a new teddy bear or healing for a cut knee. But as we mature both physically and spiritually, we begin to pray in a different vein. We pray in behalf of our family, loved ones, and neighbors. Then, when we've really begun to catch the magnitude of miracles a prayer life can bring, we find we can even pray for strangers: the man on the curb waiting for the light to change, the lady in front of us at the post office, the truck driver behind us on the highway. They all become fascinating subjects to talk over with the Lord.

Secret prayer for others, all during the day, is the acid test of our unselfishness. Self must fade out to clear a channel through which God's warmth can flow unhindered in lovely, unending prayer. To me, it seems, the highest form of communication is not asking God for things for ourselves, but letting Him flow through us, out, and over the world to others.

You might find, as I have, that when you are praying for a friend the friend may be completely closed towards God, yet open to you. By praying for this friend, you can open her toward God. In a diagram, it looks like this.

God hears, and then

I pray;

He helps
my friend.

Because of my prayer, God speaks to my friend and the friend feels the first faint desire for God and slowly opens toward Him. Up to this point there has been a wall between my friend and God, but then comes the connecting arrow of prayer and my friend is reached.

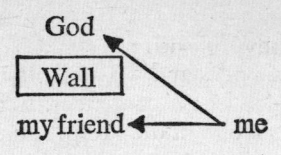

Prayer crumbles the wall.

In another manner of speaking, if you help turn a friend toward God by prayer, you perform the same service as a telephone operator. You connect the friend with God. That helps God to speak directly, person-to-person, with that friend. (How beautiful the ways of prayer.)

At the beginning of this chapter, I shared some of the prayer concepts of my mother, whose prayer life was quite astonishing. I'd like to include one more "happening," for it involves this last point of praying for others.

On the day doctors discovered the first lumps on one breast, my mother's appointment was in the morning. By evening, she was in the hospital. Surgery was performed the next morning, the breast removed, and the whole thing was over incredibly fast.

I thought she probably didn't have time to jot down a note to me, as she always did before vacation trips or hospital visits, so I didn't expect one. But three years after the surgery, she died, and tucked away in one of her notebooks I found *the* note. It was not written to me, which explains why I never got it. Instead, it was a prayer she had penned the morning of that first doctor's appointment, after reading her morning devotions. At the top of the page is the Scripture reference, Romans 12:1. The passage deals with sacrifice or giving one's whole body to the Lord. Just under the reference she wrote,

Lord,

You may do with me what You please. You may take this body and do with it as You desire. It is Your body; I now present it to Thee, and it's Yours from this moment on. Help Yourself to it, Lord.

I'm going to the hospital this afternoon. I am just a weak unknown handmaiden of Thine with no knowledge of what's ahead or of the acquaintance with the hungry hearts I may make there. So, here is my body, my hands, my feet, and my lips. Take them and use them for some troubled, burdened heart. Speak through my lips Thy words of light and life.

Amen.

I was astonished to find there was not one word, one line, or one mention of the surgery—nothing about the pending mastectomy or the possible diagnosis of cancer! Her only concern was for a needy stranger she might meet while hospitalized.

God answered that prayer faster than any other prayer she ever prayed. The first night after surgery she could not sleep, even though she had taken the prescribed sleeping pills. They simply did not take effect. She lay there, in the wee hours of the morning, not in any particular pain but curious as to why she was awake.

A nurse flicked her flashlight over Mother's face and said, "Why, Mrs. Miller, why are you awake at this hour?"

"Oh, I don't know, maybe I'm just awake so I can talk to you," she said.

Hearing that response, the nurse just flew out of the room without a word. Mother sensed there was something very wrong, so she began praying for the nurse.

A few hours later, the nurse returned to my mother's room. Mother asked her why she had left so suddenly and why she was so upset. For the next two hours, the nurse poured out the tragic events of that night and all that led up to it. Her marriage was all but over, everything was wrong and out of control in her life.

After she had seen Mother the first time that night, she'd received permission to go home for a few hours to try to pull herself together. The nurse described in detail her feelings as she entered her house. She casually wondered what her friend's sweater and dress were doing on the couch, but she dismissed the thought and went through the hall to the bedroom.

What she saw exploded in her brain as a shocking, unbelievable bolt of lightning, and it instantly triggered a furious rage within her. Her best friend and her husband, lying in bed, clutched each other as she yelled and screamed her fury at them. She said she wanted to kill them but had no gun so she ran out of the house, got into the car, and had driven around in a blind daze.

Finally, she made up her mind. She drove back to the hospital to give herself a lethal injection of a drug to end her life. She walked down the hall, and as she neared my mother's room, something compelled her to go in.

It was then that she stood before Mother a second time, and though she was crying and shaking violently, she asked, "Mrs. Miller, when I was here earlier, why did you say you were awake to talk to me?"

Mother told her simply that God had not let her sleep and that she'd seen no one but this nurse, so maybe she needed the Lord. She told her she had remained awake and praying for her all night.

In spite of the fact that my mother was out of surgery less than 24 hours, she talked until the morning nurse arrived for duty. Ever so lovingly, she led the night nurse to the healing hands of Jesus, the Great Physician. The girl prayed to receive Christ and put her trust in God.

For the rest of my mother's hospitalization, she counseled and prayed with the young nurse. Mother had the joy of watching as the Lord picked up the pieces of the girl's shattered soul and replaced the fragments with a brand new heart.

I wonder what miracles of beauty could be wrought in our lives and in those around us if we truly prayed for the calming beauty of prayer?

	Additional Verses:	
	Psalm 66:18, 19	secret sin
	Proverbs 1:24-28	indifference
Reasons for	Proverbs 21:13	neglect of mercy
unanswered	Proverbs 28:9	despising the law
prayers.	Isaiah 59:1-2	sin
	James 1:6-8	instability
	James 4:3	self indulgence
Conditions of	2 Chronicles 7:14	forgiveness
answered	Jeremiah 29:13	seek whole-
prayers:		heartedly
	Mark 11:24	faith
	1 John 3:22	asking in His will
	1 John 5:14	asking in His will
God hears!	Psalm 4:3	
	Psalm 18:6	
	Psalm 34:17	
	Psalm 91:15	
	Proverbs 15:29	
	1 Peter 5:7	

CHAPTER SIX

INFERIORITY: THE GREEN EYED CAT

"What would you change about women in general (if you could wave some sort of magic wand)?" I began research for this book by asking many different people that question. Here are some of the responses, and I've included a bit about who gave them, for the purpose of clarification:

1. "I'd like women to be more feminine" (a man married to a very militant woman).
2. "I'd like to put kindness into women's voices" (our son, who had just gotten off work at the grocery store and was tired of cranky girl checkers).
3. "I'd like women to fix up their outward looks and go on diets" (a young man married two years to a girl who seems to need exactly that).
4. "I'd like women to stop being so petty about situations involving co-workers" (my husband, an exasperated bank vice-president, who had spent several hours resolving a dispute between two women employees over a 10-minute discrepancy about lunch schedules).
5. "I'd like to open women's eyes to the world around them" (Pat French, owner of a modeling and charm school. She also mentioned that some women's thought processes were about as deep as a "Texas mud puddle").
6. "I'd like girls to stop knocking themselves" (a young, unmarried, male checker at the grocery

store. He'd just had a date with a "really beautiful" girl who was "well built," and each time he told her how great she looked, she had *denied* it).

7. "I'd like women to be outspoken and talk more" (This one really puzzled me until I realized this man is married to an absolutely gorgeous angel who has a quiet, gentle nature. He doesn't know what he's got!)

8. "I'd like women to be less critical" (a young woman who had just returned from two hours at a baby shower).

9. "I'd like women to quit trying to impress their boss and just be their original selves" (a principal of a school which employs 15 women teachers).

10. "I wish women would stop saying, 'I'm *just* a housewife,' in the same tone of voice they use to describe common constipation" (me, because I believe there is no such thing as "just a housewife").

I talked with many more people on this question, and, while the answers varied with their life-style or marital status, one common thread ran through all. In one way or another, directly or indirectly, they wanted women to get rid of their low estimate of themselves.

Nothing will wreck your ability to be a successful woman of God, to be a creative person, or to get along with others more than feeling you have little value. Accepting ourselves is one of the main hinges on the door to accepting others. What we think of ourselves influences all our actions and responses toward others.

The one who summarized all the answers best was Dr. James Dobson, who wrote me as follows:

If I could write a prescription for the women of the world, it would provide each one of them with a healthy dose of self-esteem and personal worth (taken three times a day until the symptoms disappear). I have no doubt that this is their greatest need.

The wise doctor has said it very well! The basic lack of self-worth is what we'd all like to change, and he has put his finger on the pulse of the problem when he says, ". . . this is their greatest need."

Let's look at the origins of a poor self-image, what it creates along the way of life, and what it eventually produces in our personalities.

1. *Lack of a sense of worth is rooted in our past.*

When did your low opinion of yourself begin? Probably when you were a baby. Incredible as that sounds, think about it.

You're shopping in the grocery store, and you pass a couple holding a baby in one of those infant-seat carriers. If the baby is cute, pretty, or absolutely darling, you find yourself talking, cooing, and verbally showering it with love and acceptance. "Oh, my, what a darling! What a sweetie-pie you are." You go on and on because you just *love* babies. . . or do you?

Not five minutes later, in the parking lot, a mother holding her baby walks toward you. Once more you get all enthused about babies . . . until you *see* the baby. His head is slightly enlarged, and is covered with unruly, dirty hair. His look is not alert but dull, and his face is misshaped and homely. You quickly turn the other way. You say nothing at all.

I feel almost certain that the latter baby knows he's been silently, nonverbally rejected. He is quickly learning from mere vibrations that there is something not quite acceptable about him. He is already experiencing the painful first feelings of insecurity.

Look at your own life for a moment, and think back with me. What were you teased about in your early life at home or in school? Was it your red hair or freckles, your buckteeth or oversized nose, your fatness or your skinniness, your stickout ears or the space between your two front teeth, or was it your lisping or stuttering problem? Whatever it was, very few of us have escaped the cutting wounds of childhood remarks.

The teasing that contributed the most to my feelings of inferiority was always about my thinness. I know every horrid joke about thin people that has ever been devised and uttered. I wish I had a nickel for all the times I was called "bird legs" or referred to as "skinny as a pole." The advice to "put a little meat on your bones" was given me often during those days.

I was physically a little late in maturing, and in our worship-the-bosom culture, I found gym classes particularly disturbing. I had rheumatic fever when I was 10 and never took regular physical education classes in high school. I had "rest" instead. Why I had to suit up in shirt and shorts for "rest" is still beyond me, and how I managed always to be assigned a locker next to a girl who had a build like Raquel Welch, I'll never understand! (I won't even go into the matter of taking those awful see-all-of-everybody gym showers!)

School is not the only place our self-worth is whittled down; home life can be just as destructive. Our families can contribute a great deal to our feeling of worthlessness.

A mother tells a girl often enough that she's clumsy and the daughter becomes quite good at being clumsy. Or, parents allow children to destructively criticize each other. (We need to teach not only ourselves to stop knocking each other, but our children as well.)

Sometimes parents do what we've done in the parking lot with the homely baby; they just turn the other way and ignore the child. When the child ends up in some violent kind of struggle later on, the parent says "I don't know how this happened. I love him and I've done my best." They feel that because they've never openly criticized or commented on the child, the child doesn't know their true feelings. But the parents' silence has very loudly communicated their disapproval, disappointment, or their feelings of rejection toward that child, and he knows. My *how* he knows!

I meet too many grown women who are still handicapped by some action or word of their parents.

One young wife tearfully recounts her twelfth Christmas, when her mother took a temporary job to buy presents. The mother is still, after 20 years, at that "temporary" job. "We did get a lot of nice presents," the woman continued, "but in the meantime we lost my sister to the world of drugs."

One woman cannot ever remember her mother hugging her, kissing her, or saying, "I love you."

A mother of four children recalls that her mother repeatedly told her, "You can't do *anything* right!" Then, she added that since she couldn't get along with her four kids, apparently her mother was right.

Another woman has a hard time relating to the opposite sex because all she knows about men is that her father spent his every waking moment yelling at her for something.

One woman remembers being introduced all her life by a tactless, thoughtless mother who said, "This is Jane, our little red-headed monster."

I am not qualified or capable to begin to assess the damage that has already been inflicted on these women. I am not prepared to comment on the colossal ignorance of any parent who would yoke a child with all kinds of painful burdens, but I do believe that as a mother and a parent, I stand before God and must answer to Him for all charges of parental irresponsibility.

As we move on into adulthood, we take the insecurities from our past with us. We have our ups and downs, but some of us are down often and for long periods of time. We wonder why.

2. *Lack of a sense of worth is depression's basic requirement.*

Here is part of the answer. Located at the very source of our down period is the lack of self-esteem. We all suffer from it.

I find depression in people everywhere. It seems to come in varying degrees from a casual "I've got the blahs," to the deadly calm of a person teetering on the edge of suicide. It comes in all ages, and one unbelievable time I saw it in a baby.

I was on a speaking engagement for the U.S. Army overseas, and when I finished I was asked to go to the back of the auditorium to meet a young couple. Before I was halfway down the aisle, I spotted the two very obviously depressed people and their baby.

The couple had been profoundly moved (and more than a little upset) by what I had shared relative to marriage. They had identified completely with the factors that had broken our marriage and had experienced the same sins, anger, and rebellion in their marriage. They listened as I told how God moved in our lives and then in our marriage, but they would not bring themselves to trust the Lord. They were very angry at each other and at the world in general, and were both deeply depressed. What hit me hardest was the realization that nowhere was their depression more clearly reflected than in the face of their 10-month-old son.

He sat quietly enough on his father's lap, but all his parents' ugliness and dissatisfaction was clearly visible on his little face.

Because they had identified so closely with my story, the air between us was charged with a bit of emotional tension. To give some relief to the moment, I reached over, touched the baby's cheek, and said, "Hi, Sweetie." He was so unhappy and his face so homely that it made my heart ache. In order to swallow the lump in my throat, I tried to make conversation. So, as cheerfully as possible, I said, "What's the baby's name?"

The father never looked up. He just said, in the most degrading tone of voice, "His name is Boy."

I thought that name was only used in Old Tarzan movies, so I said, "Boy?" I still couldn't believe anyone would give their son that name.

"Yes, Boy. That's *all* he is—Boy," the father repeated in a disgusted, impatient way.

I wonder what effect the name "Boy" will have on this child as he grows up? Will he be quiet and seemingly well behaved in school? Will his parents and teachers remember him as a "good" boy? Will they be unbelievably shocked when, at some later date, this young son's depression and feelings of worthlessness turn into an angry rage and he cries out to be heard by committing a horrendous act of violence? I wonder.

When I asked Dr. Dobson, a psychologist, about depression and the lack of a feeling of worth in women, he said this:

> In a questionnaire I recently administered to young, Christian mothers, their most common source of depression was clearly 'low self esteem.' On a broader scale, this painful devaluation provides the energy (and the anger) that powers the Women's Liberation Movement and other attempts to change the role of today's women. If women felt genuinely respected in their role as wives and mothers, they would not need to abandon it for something better. If they felt *equal* with men in personal worth, they would not need to be *equivalent* to men in responsibility. If they could only bask in the dignity and status granted them by the Creator, then their femininity would be valued as their greatest asset, rather than scorned as an old garment to be discarded. Without question, the future of a nation depends on how it sees its women. I hope we will teach our little girls to be glad they were chosen by God for the special pleasures of womanhood.

3. *Lack of a sense of worth makes a woman's thoughts and speech suspicious, negative, and critical.*

The woman with little sense of personal worth sees her life and the world around her through dark tinted glasses. Nothing is really good, and nothing turns out right for her. What's more, she is sure everyone else wears the same dark glasses.

One such woman told me, and she was serious (*Boy*, was she serious!), that every time she went to church people "talked bad" about her.

"The minute I sit down they start whispering about me!" she said.

"What do they say?" I asked.

Her only answer was, "All lies, lies, lies!"

Because she had no self-esteem, she was sure everywhere she went (especially church) people were against her, out to get her, and telling lies about her.

This kind of woman is so *sure* no one will like her (she doesn't like herself, so how *could* anyone else like her) that if you walk up to her and say hello she freezes like a popsicle right before your eyes. She's thinking, "Oh, she shouldn't want to speak to me . . ."

When you do speak to her, she's immediately suspicious of your motives and wonders why you are prying into her life by asking questions.

Take her on a vacation to Mexico and she's sure the bottled water is contaminated.

Take her to the best seafood restaurant on the waterfront and she complains about the "fishy smell in here."

Ask her how her work is coming and be prepared for the worst possible report.

Compliment her on her dress and she will tell you (1) how old it is (2) how much she paid for it, and (3) how she's always hated it.

Tell her you like the way she's fixed her hair and she will tell you her nose is too big or too long or her face is too fat or too narrow. (The funny thing is, you never noticed before, but from now on, whenever you see her, those irregularities will probably be the only thing you see.)

If she wants you to come over to her house for dinner, she never attacks it straight on. She says, "You wouldn't want to come over for dinner, would you?"

In the first chapter of *Ms Means Myself*,* Gladys

*Zondervan Publishing House, Grand Rapids, Mich.

Hunt talks of women like this one I've just described, women who are all hemmed in by their lack of a sense of worth.

> . . . some women are like tightly closed buds, atrophying on the vine. Afraid to open up, they do not dare risk the bloom lest it be less beautiful than someone else's.

Others become harping critics, quick to point out error in someone else and slow to love. Others don't criticize, they just internalize, never letting anyone know who they really are. They don't risk exposure or love or acceptance. Some play games, wearing the mask of a role they have chosen, sometimes a very spiritual role. Those are outwardly pious and inwardly barren, still unknown to anyone else or themselves. Others talk too much, skirting all the issues which might reveal their real person. And still others become authorities on any subject, even Bible quotes, to hide blatant insecurities.

In a negative, critical woman, it's her tongue that gives her away. It reflects all the inner workings of her heart.

> "The boneless tongue, so small and weak, can crush and kill," declares the Greek.
>
> "The tongue destroys a greater horde," the Turk asserts, "than does the sword."
>
> "The tongue can speak a word whose speed," says the Chinese, "outstrips the steed."
>
> While Arab sages this impart; "The tongue's great storehouse is the heart."
>
> From Hebrew wit and maxim sprung, "Though feet may slip, ne'er let the tongue."
>
> The sacred writer crowns the whole, "Who keeps his tongue, doth keep his soul."
>
> *(Writer unknown)*

The tongue is not the only problem. Something else is deeply affected by our insecurities.

4. *Lack of a sense of worth changes the pitch and intonation of the voice.*

Somehow, almost mysteriously, when a woman is sure she is nothing or "just a housewife," something happens to her vocal chords. Everything that's uttered from the larynx seems to be pre-set on a whining, pitying, and nagging pitch.

It's a beautiful day. You dash into the choir room on Sunday morning, grab your robe and music, and say to the first soprano you meet, "Hi, good morning—how are you this gorgeous day?!?"

Her whole face sags, and she sniffs and whimpers, "Oh, I've got the blahs, I guess."

Her whining tone is familiar because you remember hearing it in your children when they were age three. From then on, nothing you say to her cheers her up or turns her on to a more enthusiastic day. The conversation just sputters out of words and dies.

Matthew Henry said, "They who complain most are most to be complained of."

The woman who whined about her "blahs" awakened to the same beautiful day I did, but she let her sense of worthlessness overshadow and darken the entire morning. She is very uptight about the extra pounds she's gained around her waistline, and it's her personal waterloo. But it seems to be the summation of all her inner thoughts. "I'm fat." That's all she thinks of, so when someone innocently says hi to her, there is no way she can put down her insecurities and simply answer the question without whining or showing the blahs.

Madame Lola Montez, who lived in the 1800s, said,

> "One of the most powerful auxiliaries of beauty is a fine, well trained voice. Indeed, one of the most fascinating women I ever knew had scarcely any other charm to recommend her. She was a young countess in Berlin, who had dull eyes, a

rough skin, with dingy complexion, coarse dull hair and a dumpy frame. But she had an exquisite voice, which charmed everybody who heard it (*The Arts and Secrets of Beauty*, cited earlier.)

If only my soprano friend would reevaluate her true self-worth, accept her weight or go on a diet, perhaps others would notice that she's got a marvelous speaking and singing voice.

Nagging is another by-product of a poor self-image. It almost always destroys the nagger and the nagged. The nagger is so unhappy with herself that she continually looks for loop holes and flaws in others to soothe her feelings of worthlessness.

The destructive quality of nagging reaches a long way and lingers a long time.

My brother, Cliff, had a man teacher in grammar school who spent two semesters nagging him. I wish I knew what insecurities were at the bottom of this man's remarks to Cliff. Perhaps he could have been helped. But he almost destroyed my brother by picking on him and nagging him.

Of all the thousands of words teachers spoke to Cliff, he remembers most clearly this teacher and his nagging. A year's nagging was summed up in these words, "Cliff, you're so dumb and stupid, you'll never make it through high school—much less college! Why don't you just drop out of school and watch "Popeye" on TV?"

The remarks killed all Cliff's incentive to learn, and only after many years (and some war experiences in Vietnam) did Cliff reestablish a better self-image and go back to studies.

I'd love to tell this teacher the "dumb and stupid" boy not only made it through high school, he just received his master's degree, made the list of "Who's Who in Colleges," and presently is earning his doctorate!

5. *Lack of a sense of worth convinces women that*

the grass is greener on the other side of the fence and that everyone but her has it made!

We all have to cope with disillusionment and sometimes find ourselves in a sober or bad mood. But according to Dr. Theodore I. Rubin, writing in the *Ladies Home Journal,* "Acute disillusionment generates more serious depression and self-hate, and can even lead to suicide. Disillusionment is never possible without fantasy. . . ."

Fantasy is no stranger to most of us, and early in childhood we begin to know we live in two worlds—the real and the imagined. Many times our fantasies become a way of handling our insecurities and problems. One woman said, "I used to spend hours aching, dreaming of the kind of mother I so wished I had."

When we permit ourselves to live in a fantasy world, we rob ourselves of the opportunity to see God at action in our real world. It becomes very difficult to separate the facts from fantasy, and then we really have problems.

Looking at and comparing the success of others, the beauty of others, the brains of others, and the wealth of others with our own can lead to the biggest fantasy of all. Feelings of low self-worth and jealousy join with the spirit of covetousness to push us straight down the road toward Depressionville.

See how many of the following statements you've heard lately.

"I don't have any talents. Mrs. Jones just makes me sick because she's got so many!"

"That may work for Sue. She relates well to people, but I don't, so I won't accept the nomination."

"You should see the mansion Beverly just moved into. She's got more bathrooms than I've got rooms in my whole house."

"Naturally, if I looked as beautiful as Clare, I'd be radiant and charming too!"

"You don't know what it's like to try to live off a pension check each month. You're loaded with money."

"Well, if I was married to Harry, I'd be a terrific wife too. I'd like to see her married to my George for six months. She'd never make it."

"You kids are driving me crazy. I've tried to be a good mother, but how come you don't act like the Brown's kids?"

David knew all about this kind of wishful fantasizing. If you have a *Living Bible*, read the entire 73rd Psalm. Here are just a few statements from that chapter to give you new insights on an old problem.

"For I was envious of the prosperity of the proud and wicked. Yes, all through life their road is smooth! They grow sleek and fat. They aren't always in trouble and plagued with problems like everyone else. . . . These fat cats have everything their hearts could ever wish for!" (vv. 3-7)

It was Shakespeare who wrote in *Othello*, "O! Beware, my lord, of jealousy; it is the green-eyed monster which doth mock the meat it feeds on."

David, later in the 73rd Psalm, decided to go to God's sanctuary and spend some time meditating about his jealous feelings. He concludes, "Their [evil men's] present life is only a dream!" (v. 20)

Still later he states. "I saw myself so stupid and so ignorant; I must seem like an animal to You, O God. But even so, You love me!" (vv. 22, 23)

I'll stop there but the 73rd Psalm goes on to a magnificent conclusion. I hope you'll finish it. Each time I read that chapter, I come away just breathless because of David's words to the Lord, "But even so, You love me."

Herein lies the key to overcoming the low self-esteem you may be experiencing. It begins with realizing, "But even so, You love me."

The woman who picks and claws at the beauty or success of others is most ugly.

The woman who indulges in fantasies is living in an unrealistic, imaginary world. She misses the intoxicating joy of real living.

The woman of little self-worth who continually

longs to have someone else's looks, husband, talent, or house is pathetically misusing her time here on earth. Her life is a monumental waste of effort and energy, particularly in view of what it could be. She slides deeper into the quicksand of depression and does not see the solid, outstretched hand of God. She bypasses all He had planned for her, and she completely misses His words when He says, "My dear child, grab hold of Me, take My hand and I'll pull you out. I'll set you free. You are very precious to Me, and I have come to rescue you. Take My hand. Come unto Me. I love you."

If you have identified in any way with the woman of low self-esteem, you can change that. You can lift your level, upgrade your position, and raise your own sense of worth by starting here and now. Realize first that: God is pouring out His love upon you right now, this very second.

Then, read on. There's more.

Additional verses:

Psalm 73
Isaiah 40:28, 31, 32
Hebrews 4:13, 15
1 Corinthians 1:20, 21
1 Corinthians 2:11, 12
2 Corinthians 9:8
2 Corinthians 5:17

CHAPTER SEVEN

THE POISED BEAUTY OF SELF-ACCEPTANCE

Yesterday the Rev. David Ray, pastor of the Valley Community Church of San Dimas, Calif., interviewed me for one of his television specials. He was talking with me about my book *To Lib Or Not To Lib,** and we discussed some of the ways a woman becomes a person because of Christ.

Toward the end of the interview, Mr. Ray asked me to name some of the positive characteristics found in women and in womanhood today.

I felt a little overwhelmed because the interview was coming to a close and it's hard to dash off an answer to such a large question.

I'm glad I don't have a time limit here so we can really look at a few of those characteristics in depth.

It seems to me there are three very basic attributes prevalent in a poised, beauty-filled Christian woman. The three traits connect, and interrelate to a woman's self-concept.

It all begins by a woman realizing her worth in God's sight—not hers. If she has accepted herself as God has accepted her, that concept becomes the very pulsebeat of her life. It is the inner "thump, thump, thump" that says, "She's alive, she's alive, she's alive!" God thought her so valuable that He laid down His life to reach her and to save her. If she really knows this, her whole life glows with this first trait.

*Victor Books, Wheaton, Ill., 1972.

1. *She has accepted God's forgiveness and His evaluation of her.*

Gladys Hunt* feels so strongly about the problems of a low self-image that she writes:

> I am increasingly convinced that a major cause of the despondency, the ineffectual living, the lack of freedom, the feeling of worthlessness so common in today's world is a failure to understand what God has done in redeeming us—and how and why He has done it.

When a woman begins to understand that God has forgiven her and actually accepts His forgiveness, fantastic things happen! She escapes the confining cocoon of a non-person and explodes into the sunshine of personhood as a real woman!

However, when a woman asks God to forgive her but then refuses (for one reason or another) to accept that forgiveness, a shroud of frustration envelopes her life. She does not think of herself as a child of God, so she lives out her existence in loneliness like some poor forgotten orphan.

John said, "But to all who received Him, He gave the right to become children of God" (John 1:12).

Some women have never realized, capitalized on, or utilized the right to become God's children. I find that sad and completely unnecessary. John must have given it some thought too, because immediately he adds, "All they needed to do was trust Him to save them."

Some women tell me they can't accept God's forgiveness because their particular sins are too many or too big. They completely forget that God is not shocked by their sins because He already knows all about them!

One of the most beautiful verses in the Word of God tells us that God, who knows all, loved us any-

*Op. cit.

way. "Long ago, even before He made the world, God chose us to be His very own, through what Christ would do for us; He decided then to make us holy in His eyes, without a single fault, we who stand before Him covered with His love" (Eph. 1:4).

The next time you hear someone say they can't believe or accept the fact that God has forgiven them, tell them this:

"Yes, it is true that when you stand before the Lord
    to ask His forgiveness,
Your dress is ragged and tattered because of ugly
    sins,
Your hair is thickly tangled with the webs of rebellion,
Your shoes are torn and muddied by your past failures.

But God never sees any of that!

He sees you holy,
And He sees you perfect,
Because you are dressed in His righteousness,
And He has covered you with the full-length cape
    of His love.
He sees nothing else!
Even when you explain how you really look underneath, He hears, but He forgets forever.
The dimension of His forgetfulness is as far as the
    East is from the West,
And it endures past all of eternity!"

Peter also reveals our worth in God's sight when he says, "Dear friends, God the Father chose you long ago and knew you would be His children." (1 Peter 1:2).

Just think:

You have come from God.
You belong to God.
You are important to God.
You will return to God.

Fortunately, God does not evaluate us by society's standards. He does not hold up a beauty chart and check off our measurements or compare our statistics. He does not require us to take periodic I.Q. tests to reveal our degree of intelligence. He does not examine our Dun and Bradstreet credit report to see what we have accomplished financially. God is not hampered, in any way, by this world's cockeyed value system. He sees us as already perfect in Christ.

David makes this quite clear when he writes, "O God, You have declared me perfect in Your eyes. . . ." (Ps. 4:1). This verse, just by itself, would be an important one in accepting God's forgiveness, but there's a lot more to it than that.

How could David have written in one place that God had declared him perfect and written in another, "O, Lord, you have examined my heart and know everything about me" (Ps. 139:1)?

My mind boggles a bit when I think of the total picture the Scriptures have given us about David. If we are not too familiar with David, we generally think of him only in terms of the mighty warrior and slayer of Goliath, writer of the Psalms, and famous king of all Israel. However, the other side of his life, the human and very weak traits of his character, tend to remind us of a television Peyton Place soap opera. By our standards, David didn't come too close to winning "Best King of the Year" award some years.

If there was any person in all of history who had a right to feel more worthless than David, I can't imagine who it would be. Consider these sins and failures.

1. He committed adultery.
2. He committed murder.
3. He was highly joyous one day and deeply depressed the next.
4. Absalom, an older son, murdered his brother.
5. David failed as a father.
6. David failed in communicating to his wives.

I'm so glad the Bible gives us a clear picture of him. Otherwise, we might have said, "Look at David, the handsome, famous, talented king of Israel. No wonder he was so great. He had no problems, and no hang-ups."

God "knew everything" about him, yet declared him perfect!

After David admitted God's all-knowing power (in Ps. 139:1) he does a second thing; he thanks God for making him the way he is (Ps. 139:14). That included thanking God for his disadvantages as well as for his talents and great characteristics.

Have you ever tried thanking God for the handicaps in your life, those disturbing childhood memories, that wart on your nose, or that limp in your walk? It is never easy, but it can be done when we remember God only sees us in our perfect state. He sees the finished product of our lives; the wart never shows up in His view finder. Thank God for your life, because God's value system says you are beautiful! (I'll write more in depth on thanking God in a later chapter.)

Thirdly, David has shot his arrow right on target by writing the four-letter word *will* over and over.

"O Lord I *will* praise you . . ."
"I *will* bless the Lord . . ."
"I *will* cry unto the Lord . . ."
"I *shall* be joyful . . ."
"I *will* abide . . ."
"I *will* sing . . ."
"I *will* trust . . ."

David, knowing all the inner facets of his life, made living a matter of his will. In view of his sins and failures, it makes sense to conjecture that David must not have *felt* like

praising,
blessing,
thanking,
singing, or
abiding,

but he did not leave it up to how he felt. He dropped his feelings, he turned from them and lived by a decision of his will. In short, he made up his mind! We always tend to underestimate the power of our minds.

Personally, I think women are more gifted in displaying and using will power than men. When a woman sets her mind to doing something, you can count on it being done. She has a fantastic gift for making up her mind if she wants to!

It was the great Henrietta Mears who best caught the power of using our will and making up our minds when she stated,

> Will is the whole man active. I cannot give up my will; I must exercise it. I must will to obey. When God gives a command or a vision of truth, it is never a question of what He will do, but what we will do. To be successful in God's work is to fall in line with His will and to do it His way. All that is pleasing to Him is a success.*

Think of a strong, vibrant, godly woman who has just lost her husband. We go to her to give comfort and we come away comforted. We reach out to help her and we receive blessings instead. Whenever this happens, you can be sure that somewhere along the line she has dropped *how she feels* at the moment of her highest grief and has *made up her mind* to accept this loss and say, "What do You want me to learn from this, Father?" We stand in awe of this woman; yet what she has done should be the norm, not the exception, for a Christ-centered woman.

Somewhere I read, "The Lord gave us two ends to use—one to sit with and one to think with. Our success depends on which end we use the most. Heads we win, tails we lose."

Another woman is still whipping herself for failures and sins committed 35 years ago. She's simply not using her correct end! She forgets every present joy.

Henrietta Mears and How She Did It!, Ethel May Baldwin, Regal Books, Glendale, Calif., 1966.

The fact that God has given her one blessing after another completely escapes her. She has no sense of worth; she cannot take God's forgiveness; and she let's how she feels direct her entire life. The sad part is that after so many years of letting her guilt feelings, her sad feelings, her failure feelings, dictate her waking hours, she can no longer *use* her mind. She can't really make up her mind about anything. Even the simple task of deciding on baked or mashed potatoes has become an enormous chore.

If this woman went to a psychiatrist or a psychologist, she could pay up to $100 an hour to hear him say, almost word for word, what Paul said a long time ago, "Accept life, and be most patient and tolerant with one another, always ready to forgive if you have a difference with anyone." (Col. 3:12, Phillips)

The doctor would probably tell her to accept her life, her past failures, and her unhappy childhood. He'd advise her of what her bitterness is doing to her. If he were a Christian doctor, he'd talk about forgiving God, forgiving others, forgiving herself, and forgiving circumstances. He'd try to get her to thank God even in these present moments, and he'd convince her to use her mind in a constructive way.

When we put our inferiority feelings away and make living, praising, and singing a matter of the will, we really awaken our sleepy, run-down minds. Don't be discouraged if your mind is slow to cooperate. Keep at it, because Paul says, "But strange as it seems, we Christians actually do have within us a portion of the very thoughts and mind of Christ!" (1 Cor. 2:16). Think about the power of having the "mind of Christ" within our minds!

It was Toki Miyashina who made this paraphrase of the 23rd Psalm. Read it aloud, for it will help prepare you for achieving the first trait found in the poised beauty of self-acceptance.

The Lord is my pacesetter,
    I shall not rush;

He makes me stop and rest
   for quiet intervals.
He provides me with images of stillness
   which restore my serenity.
He leads me in ways of efficiency
   through calmness of mind
And His guidance is peace.
Even though I have a great many
   things to accomplish each day,
   I will not fret;
For His presence is here.
His timelessness, His all importance
   will keep me in balance.
He prepares refreshment and renewal
   in the midst of my activity.
By anointing my mind with His oils of tranquility
   my cup of joyous energy overflows.
>   Surely harmony and effectiveness
>   shall be the fruits of my hours
>   For I shall walk in the pace of my Lord
>   and dwell in His house forever.

The trait I've just discussed, of accepting God's forgiveness and His evaluation, has everything to do with our vertical relationship to God. This next trait goes out from us, horizontally, toward others. Sometimes our ability to reach out to others (or the degree of success involved) is sharply curtailed by our low self-estimate and our obsession with *"My problem."*

The woman who has accepted God's forgiveness in her life and has begun to thank Him for each and every aspect of her life should lose her critical tongue, and she will, if she glows with the next trait.

2. *She has developed the no-knock policy in all relationships.*

My friend Dr. Dobson once said, "People who feel inferior—talk about it."

The most critical of all people, as I mentioned in the previous chapter, are the ones who have little or no feelings of worth. They are terribly preoccupied with "poor me" attitudes. Sometimes they are unaware of others in their own families who are bleeding and crying for help. Often they become extremely critical (vocally) towards everyone. They feel such a failure in what they are doing that they cannot accept someone else's success.

My husband is always being asked how it feels to be married to the "famous" Joyce Landorf. His self-image is so balanced by the Lord that Dick is not threatened in any way by any type of success I might achieve. When he is sometimes introduced as Mr. Joyce Landorf, it does not wound his ego because his ego is surrendered to the Lord and his self-worth is God established, not man established. He is a man in his own right and in God's sight. He is not only unthreatened by my speaking, singing, and writing successes, but he is my most inspiring encouragement! (I could do none of these things without his full, approving love.) I can truthfully say he is rarely critical of *anyone*.

There is definitely something you can do to break the negative pattern of your conversation if you have honestly admitted that you are critical of others a good deal of the time.

It was Dr. Dobson who first suggested that we need to develop the "no-knock policy." I hope he'll forgive me for plagiarizing his phrase, but it's been one of the most helpful suggestions I've ever heard. When he first talked about the no-knock policy, I jolted upright in my chair because I was instantly reminded that I had "knocked" myself three times that very evening! They were small digs at my abilities and, while it did not hurt anyone else, it clearly revealed the feelings of inadequacy that were on my mind. It also told me I had said those negative things about myself in hopes that someone else would say, "Oh, no, Joyce, you are wrong about yourself . . ." and then they would praise me in the process.

Yesterday a young mother was telling about an incident she'd had with her children and she said, "There I was, dumb, stupid me, standing . . ." Then, not two minutes later she added, "Well, you know, I'm such a screwball and so disorganized, I . . ."

Our conversation was interrupted, and I was sorry I had no opportunity to talk to her about the no-knock policy.

Adopting the no-knock policy works like this: Everytime you would say something negative or critical about yourself, your mate, your children, your neighbor, friends, business acquaintances, anyone, you refuse to say it. You crush it while it's still in the thought stage.

Remember, you are going to answer to God not for anyone else's actions, words, or deeds, just yours. So, your critical, harmful opinions do nothing but slam back rather hard on you. Forget your bad past and bury your last year's failures, accept forgiveness for your life, and command your tongue to silence.

Peter says, "So get rid of your feelings of hatred. Don't pretend to be good. Be done with dishonesty and jealousy and talking about others behind their backs." (1 Peter 2:1)

Hard to do? You bet! Some of us have been habitually critical for years, and the habit will be hard to break.

If you could play back a tape of all your conversations covering the past four weeks, what would the percentages of critical comments total? Would 30% be the sum and total of all derogatory remarks about yourself and others? Or would 50% of your sentences be negative statements about someone? I have asked myself these questions, and I was alarmed at the facts and percentages in my personal life.

Proverbs 11:17 says, "Your own soul is nourished when you are kind; it is destroyed when you are cruel."

I do not want to stand by and see the beauty of my soul or yours be destroyed by this disfiguring habit. We must exercise this no-knock policy in dealing with ourselves. We must practice this policy toward our husbands and if we want to teach it to our children, we must practice the no-knock policy on them. They learn much more by catching than teaching.

Drop, abandon, and abolish phrases like:
"Billy is my two-year-old monster."
"Sue certainly is a scrawny little thing."
"You always make me mad."
"You spoiled brat; stop that!"

My mother was 45 years old when she gave birth to my sister, Marilyn, but (to her everlasting credit) I never heard her introduce my sister by, "This is Marilyn, our little surprise package. Ha! Ha!" or, "Meet Marilyn, our little caboose. Ha! Ha!" She would not degrade or knock her children publicly or privately.

We must specifically train our children not to knock themselves, their brothers or sisters, or us.

The night Dr. Dobson talked about adopting the no-knock policy, our daughter, Laurie, had driven me to the meeting. During a mid-evening break, I was talking to a woman when Laurie came up behind me. The seating area was cramped and there was only a narrow aisle. When Laurie passed me, she lightly patted me on the hips and gaily whispered, "My, we're spreading out a little here, aren't we?"

It was no big deal, but I'd turned 40 and for the first time in my life I weighed 115 pounds (and I wasn't pregnant). I laughed at the moment, but on the drive home I told Laurie that I knew I was being silly and immature but that her remark had stung a little. She didn't say too much but we talked about adopting the no-knock policy.

The next night, during the break, Laurie handed me this note.

Mom, I'm really sorry I teased you about being big in the hips. I do want you to know, you look beautiful tonight, and you truly are a beautiful woman. I want to strive to be the wife and mother you are to Dad, Rick, and me. (I think that's terrible wording, but I'm sure you understand what I mean.) You are what I will be someday . . . a fascinating woman. I love you, Mom.

It was an appropriate lesson for both of us. (Besides, I made up my mind to do daily exercises and take off inches in the hip area. It took two months, but, you know, when a woman makes up her mind. . . .")

The third trait of a poised woman indirectly involves her mind but more directly concerns her body and physical posture.

3. *She has learned to walk tall.*

When a woman is in the right relationship with God, when she is allowing the Holy Spirit to control and work in her life, she walks spiritually like a giant. When you talk with her, God will speak through her to you. You are impressed by His presence when you see her.

Dr. Billy Graham called Henrietta Mears "one of the greatest Christians I have ever known." I felt exactly the same way. I knew her only the last four years of her life, but she was a giant. I am 5′ 6″ tall and I looked down at Miss Mears, but the second she spoke, I had to look up—way up. Always she turned my eyes off her face and up to Jesus. It was an uncanny thing. She was a real person, humorous and intelligent, and yet I always felt I should take my shoes off when I was around her as though I were standing on holy ground.

When Miss Mears was in a living room, the Lord was sure to be right there close. Spiritually, she walked tall, and physically (though she was not much over 5′) she walked tall and elegantly, like a beautiful, gracious queen. Everything stopped when she entered a room, and each person in the room shared the single thought, *She's here!*

By contrast, Miss Mears always entered the room not with an attitude that said, "Here I am, you lucky people, I'm what you've been waiting for!" but with astounding humility that said, "Oh, here you are! I've been looking for you. How wonderful to see you!"

There was a triumphal spring to her walk. Her posture and grooming were marvelous.

I spent my entire childhood hearing my father say, "Joyce, straighten up!" Often my mother lightly touched my shoulder blades and said one word, "Up."

Once a teacher tried to improve my posture by telling me to think of someone holding one or two strands of my hair straight up and to pretend I was being suspended from the ceiling as I walked. Another suggested I carry my bosom higher.

Then, on several occasions, I saw Miss Mears walk into a room, and each time this tiny, yet dynamic woman fascinated me. I began to study her. I discovered that she did not enter like I did, nor like anybody else, for that matter.

I usually burst or exploded into a room. I brought the hurry, fatigue, and general disappointments of the day with me. I always led my body with my head and shoulders. (I still do when I forget these lessons.)

The best advice I've ever read on posture and walking is in a chapter called, "She Walks in Beauty" from a book by Marjorie Frost.*

> Maintain your good posture every step of the way to your chair after you've entered a room. This is one of the most important times to remember to lead with your thighs, because of a tendency to lean the body way forward and to bend the knees as if sitting, thus giving a 'sitting walk' demonstration all the way to the chair.

Most of us know we are to hold our head high and relax the shoulders down but to lead with the *thighs* is a new concept. It's a great principle to walk by because it puts our whole body in a nice perpendicular line of graciousness and poise.

Miss Mears had this concept down to a fine science.

*Charming You, Zondervan Publishing House, Grand Rapids, Mich.

She brought warmth, enthusiasm, and unrestricted joy into any room by the way she simply walked into it.

Her clothes and grooming were slightly spectacular. She dressed as if she were God's daughter, as if she really believed that God, the King, was her Father. Even in her childhood, she had dresses that she only wore to God's house. I am not saying she spent enormous amounts of money on clothing, but I am saying that whatever she wore was in perfect taste and absolutely becoming to her.

Once, when she was talking about grooming, Miss Mears suggested that we, in the privacy of our bedrooms, dressing rooms, or what have you, check each detail of personal grooming. Make it as perfect as we could by checking it all out at the mirror before leaving home. Then walk out in the world and completely forget the whole thing. You don't need to be self-conscious about your looks if you have given careful attention to your grooming before you step outside. You might want to check your looks right now in a verbal mirror. Are you one of these three women?

You go to the grocery store to do your shopping dressed in your "absolute grubbies," and topping off the whole mess, your hair is rolled up in super-size pink rollers. You may not know it, but for all to clearly see is a sign above your head. It follows wherever you go and it says, "I do not like myself. I am rebelling over this stupid, boring job of buying groceries. I am showing my resentment of being a wife and of life in general by looking my ugliest!"

One high school instructor said, "I always understand why a girl is like she is after I've seen her mother at the market in rollers and hair curlers."

Or maybe this sounds familiar:

You show up at church in a dress that was designed for a 17-year-old girl who is a size 7. It's been 10 years since you've been 17, and you've never been down to a size 10, much less 7. Besides that, all the extra pounds you kept after the last baby stayed on your hips and upper thighs. Your short skirt waves around your chubby thighs like a ridiculous flag. You are a grooming disaster because you are trying to dress like someone else (a younger, junior-figured girl), and everybody but you knows it.

Or maybe you're just at home cooking dinner, but you look so untidy and unappealing that you spoil your family's appetite. You wonder why they are not happy during dinner, why they bolt their food down without conversation, and why the dinner hour is better known at your house as the "disaster hour."

None of these three women I've described have learned to walk tall. Any inner self-acceptance they may have once had has dried up and blown away. Their outward grooming, their posture, and their walk all speak of their lack of inner joy.

The woman who inwardly accepts God's forgiveness, likes herself on God's terms, and reflects the no-knock policy walks in beauty. She creates this visual picture:

She has clean and shining hair,
Her make-up is not heavy but soft and feminine,
She cares for her fingernails regularly (and beautifully).
Her teeth are clean and healthy,
She has regular medical checkups each year,
She uses a daily deodorant and radiates personal cleanliness,
Her fragrance is definite but gentle and sweet,
She exercises regularly and sticks to a diet,
Her whole wardrobe fits her budget,
She uses color to its best advantage,
Her speech is not boisterous or profane but kind.
She avoids unlady-like positions and moves with grace.

This outward appearance combines with her inner traits, and we see that she walks:

According to God's commands.   Psalm 1
Obediently.   Jeremiah 7:23

Relaxed, because she travels "a good path."	Jeremiah 6:16
In safety.	Proverbs 2:7, 8
In newness of life.	Romans 6:4
Without guilt.	Romans 8:1
With the Holy Spirit as a guide.	Galatians 6:16
With honesty.	Romans 12:3
In love, following Christ.	Ephesians 5:2
In freedom.	1 Peter 2:16

She looks ethereally lovely because of God's harmonious, well-balanced loveliness shining all about her.

She walks in flawless perfection, shimmering with the lights of His beauty.

Additional Verses:

God loved you:	Jeremiah 31:3
	Psalm 59:10
	Psalm 18:18, 19
God made you:	Acts 17:24-28
	1 Peter 4:19
God's plan for you:	Psalm 103:1, 5a, 8-10, 12, 13
	Psalm 147:5
	Ephesians 1:5, 7, 9-13
	Ephesians 2:10
	Hebrews 4:13, 15
God's walk for you:	Proverbs 13:20
	Psalm 119:5, 9
	1 John 1:7

CHAPTER EIGHT

ANGER:
MAD AS A WET HEN

I have always been aware of the inner fire burning deep inside me. It has flared and burned with varying degrees of temperature over the years.

When I was little and in grade school, I kept those fires my own, quiet secret. Whenever the angry, resentful flames flared up, I silently drowned them out with my tears. In fact, I cried so much that my father's favorite line was, "Joyce flushes easily." Each time a person or problematic circumstance frustrated me, I handled it by crying. I managed to cry my way through junior high, high school, and college.

Something happened to those fires after a few years of marriage and two children. They began to burn fiercely and, more often than I cared to admit, raged out of control. The long-quiet, smoldering coals burst forth and erupted like a forceful volcano. Besides crying, I now began spewing my anger verbally over everyone and everything.

I don't know where the phrase "mad as a wet hen" came from or exactly how it got started but I do know,

This hen,

When wet,

Gets mad!

At first I blamed it on my nationality, or rather my parents' nationalities. My mother was Hungarian and my father, Irish. Both nationalities were suitable candidates for the "hot-temper" reputation. I remember excusing my outbursts by saying with a touch of nationalistic pride, "Well, you know the Hungarians and the Irish—how could I be any other way?" (Others have blamed their red hair or their Uncle Fred.)

Sometimes I excused my hostile behavior by explaining, "It is better to get it all out into the open. Explode and get it over with." I was proud I didn't hold grudges. It never occurred to me that I had left shattered people in the wake of my tongue lashings.

After a few years of trying unsuccessfully to excuse my temperamental outbursts, I simply reverted to blaming everyone else. Not too long ago, I saw a woman who vividly reminded me of those days. I was standing in line behind her in the post office, waiting to mail a package. It was crowded and rushed because of the holiday season, and the wait was long. Just as the woman stepped up to the clerk's window, a man came in the front door, went to the side of the window, and said (over the woman's shoulder), "Hi, Bill, do you have my meter ready?"

The postman looked up, answered, "Sure, Bob!" and handed the meter to him.

The whole business took just under four seconds, but it was all that poor lady needed to explode into a furious rage. She slammed her fist down on the counter and yelled, "Who does he think he is? I was here first; I was next in line! Where does he get off—barging in front of me? I was first!"

The startled, somewhat shaken clerk put up both hands and tried to calm her by saying, "Lady, lady, it's all right. It just took a second . . ."

She leaned through the window, over the counter, and shook her finger in his face, "Who are you," she screamed, "to take his side? I was here first! I've got things to do and places to go. Just shut your mouth and give me some stamps!"

All of us in that crowded postal substation were highly amused by the ridiculous scene the woman was creating. It was really funny. Here was a grown woman jumping up and down, pounding her fist, and screaming her lungs out over such a trivial, meaningless thing.

I was smiling right along with everyone else until I very succinctly heard a still small voice within me say, "Why are you laughing at her? I have seen you act exactly the same way." The Lord's words caught my breath, and I stopped smiling.

I took a closer look at the woman who was still ranting and raving, and I felt as if I were viewing a television "instant replay" of my soul from some years back.

"I used to be that horrible, ugly lady," I thought. It's been a long time since I've exploded like that, but perhaps God let me see this angry woman to remind me of what my life used to be. Maybe I needed to remember to keep my heart sensitive and understanding to those who suffer from hostile, flaming eruptions in their souls.

I feel almost certain that woman left the post office that day, went home, and told her husband how awful she had been treated. She probably blamed everybody there for her conduct and her words.

I remember blaming everyone else too. I'd say,

"My husband was insensitive to my needs."
"My children were impossible."
"The mailman was curt and rude."
"The neighbor doesn't like me."
"That salesman cheated me."
"The bank teller started the argument."

It was never my fault. I only started screaming after someone else had provoked me. I staunchly maintained my innocence and was very defensive about the whole matter. I lived out each day in anger. I was mad at God, mad at myself, mad at others, and fit to be tied with the angry frustrations of life in general.

Anger, during those disastrous beginning years of our marriage, wrote its name across my face in hard, dark, indelible lines. It announced to the world that it was my master controller. For me, looking into a mirror was an awful thing each day because I could see the creeping ugly lines of anger aging my face. I not only feared growing old, but I was furious because I could see it happening. I was in my early 20s but my face was aging at an alarming rate!

What anger did to my looks, however, was nothing compared to the atrocities it perpetrated on my emotions and my mind. Every outburst of temper took its unbelievable toll on my character and personality.

As a woman, I became closed-minded and opinionated about everyone from the butcher to the girls in the P.T.A. I made instant judgments and assumptions on everything from convenience foods to politics. (I must have been a colossal bore!)

To our children, I became a strict, overbearing, tyrannical mother who threatened them daily with, "Don't you make me mad or I'll lose my temper and you'll be sorry!" (From ground level, I must have loomed before my children like an ugly fire-breathing mother-monster.)

But it was in the husband and wife relationship that I suffered the greatest emotional losses. During the day I became rigid and tense whenever I tried to say anything to Dick. Or I experienced the reverse of that, and the torrent of angry words just poured out. At night, I dutifully went to bed with him, but I went as an uncooperative lover, insensitive to his needs. Anger and frigidity were only the outward, visible symptoms of a hidden disease. My real problem was the sin of not being in a right relationship with God.

The last paragraphs have not been pleasant for me to remember and write down. Yet, I know some of you will read and identify with the honest description of my life and will begin, maybe for the first time, to see the unvarnished ugliness of anger.

In the middle of our fifth year of marriage, by God's timely, miraculous intervention, both Dick and I became Christians.

Then, the Lord took my anger, resentment, and flaming temper completely away. Dick and I sailed into the peaceful sunset—on our harmonious ship of matrimony—over the smooth, calm sea of contentment.

Baloney! Don't you believe that lie for one single second. Real life is not like that. Anger is real. It is an emotion you have before you accept Christ and one you still have after you accept Him. It's as natural as my being 5′ 6″ tall when I come to Christ and measuring 5′ 6″ after I've asked Him into my heart. (I may have grown taller spiritually in these years and I pray so, but at first it was plain ol' 5′ 6″ before *and* after.)

I do not believe it is wrong to experience anger. You should recognize anger as a normal, valid emotion. You can have anger, but if anger has you, then that's a different story. If anger controls you, it twists and warps every facet of your personality and that is wrong. It is sin.

I said earlier in this chapter that I had an inner fire within me. I still do, even though I've been a Christian for 15 years. I am capable of showing that fire at any time.

The charm school director, Pat French, and I were discussing anger and what place it has or does not have in Christian women. At one point she said, "I wouldn't give you two cents for a woman if she didn't have that inner fire in her." (Bless you, Pat!)

When the Lord got me, he got the inner fire too. However, in order to make Christ my Lord, Saviour, and King, I had to move the inner fires of anger off the throne of my life. I had to dethrone and devaluate my anger. It no longer could have first place in the center of my being, and it could no longer run my life or make decisions for me. It was not easy in those early days of being a Christian to objectively (and correctly) assess the damage anger had already wrought on my soul, but I began to try. I couldn't see myself, as a Christian woman, constantly losing my temper. I realized that there would be times when someone (or something) could rouse the anger in me, but blowing my top in a temper tantrum seemed to be inappropriate and in very poor taste for a woman newly born in Christ.

In looking back over the frustrations and resentments that seemed to trigger my angry outbursts, I found two very distinct kinds of anger. It is important to look carefully and prayerfully at both of them. How successfully you handle the emotion of anger may be determined by what you discover about anger's nature. One type of anger is destructive and ugly, whereas the other type can actually bring healing or creative changes. Here is the ugly type of anger.

1. *Personal anger*

This ego-shattering kind of anger always involves what someone did or said *to me*. It's always a case of *personal abuse*. For instance, I was resentful and angry because others . . .

> got the job I wanted.
> recorded albums.
> wrote books or sang solos.
> got pay raises.
> won recognition.
> were appreciated.
> looked beautiful.

I was angry and hurt because my husband and family . . .

> misunderstood my motives.
> failed to be perfect (there's a good one!).
> cramped my style.
> noticed my lack of cooking and cleaning skills.
> griped about my lack of cooking and cleaning skills.
> didn't appreciate me and told me so.

As you can see, most of my anger was the personal kind. In all fairness to myself, I must say that once in awhile I did suffer a real injustice and that I had a few honest moments of anger, but it was a rare occurrence.

My reactions to these assaults to my ego were always wild arpeggios of anger. I allowed the destructive qualities of anger to dictate my actions. My wounded pride was usually at the core of my anger.

This next type of anger is a world removed from personal anger. It is—

2. *Virtuous anger*

This anger is a loving, caring, sinless kind of emotion that involves our being angry because of an injustice or wrong done to *someone else.* If we will use this virtuous anger in a loving way, we can become true agents of reconciliation in a world that's torn and splitting apart.

That's the hang-up though. Most of us are not angry about injustices involving others. Our anger is so self-centered that we rarely get mad for someone else. As an apathetic generation, we have forgotten what bridges can be built by loving, caring, sinless anger.

One of the most enriching adventures in music I've ever had started by exercising this kind of anger.

During a Sunday morning church service, I was looking at the nearly 200 college students scattered around the balcony, and I got mad. I was angry because we had children's choirs and adult choirs but no collegiate group. There sat all those kids and all that unused potential. I was angry enough to go see our minister of music, Rollie Calkin.

After I'd poured out my concern and urgently pleaded for a college folk-rock group to be started, I finished with, "Somebody has got to do something with these college kids!"

Rollie said, "Right! *You* do it." (I had in mind Rollie's doing something, not me!)

It's been six years since I organized and directed those beautiful kids, but the group known as the "Overtones" has continued on. They've given hundreds of concerts, recorded an album or two, and have influenced hundreds of young people to trust in Christ. It all began with virtuous anger.

We tend to think of Jesus as always turning the other cheek, as being meek and mild, but that's not a complete picture. Jesus did get angry. He was very definitely "mad as a wet hen" when He threw the money changers out of the temple. But His anger was always this second kind, this virtuous kind.

Mark 3:4, 5 reveals He had enemies; He was talking to some of them in that passage. After they wouldn't answer Jesus' questions, Mark describes Jesus as "looking around at them *angrily*, for He was deeply disturbed by their indifference to human need . . ." So Jesus was angry, but Mark clearly labels the type of anger. Jesus was not angry at the people but at their attitude of indifference!

Dr. Henry Brandt helped me understand about the spirit of love and the spirit of anger. He clearly set down the principle that if I was filled with the spirit of love, nothing could make me angry. If I in turn was filled with the spirit of anger, practically anything could make me angry.

In the years that have followed, the truth of those words has become a reality. When I ask the Lord, daily, to fill me with His spirit of love, the ugly personal anger (involving ego) simply does not get a chance to work its poison. On the other hand, the sinless kind of anger (involving others) can lovingly be used in creative ways, healing and restoring as it goes along.

Only twice in those years did it not work that way. Both times the episodes involved my father and what he was doing (or not doing) to my sister. Both times my talking to him *began* quietly with sinless anger and righteous, virtuous concern on my part for my sister. Both times I failed to be the Christian I should have been. Somewhere, in both conversations, I lost (or dropped) my sinless anger concept and succumbed to personal anger. It proves that, while one may start in the spirit of love, it's possible to slip unconsciously into the control of an angry spirit.

"Don't you *ever* get mad at your children?" one mother of four asked. Of course I get mad, but I try to get mad at what they have done (the deed) and not at them (the person). If I get hung up on what they have done to me, my temper will always be simmering just below boil.

When Laurie put a single scratch down the entire length of my car, she knew I was mad. However, losing my temper, screaming and yelling, "You stupid girl, how could you have managed to scratch the entire length of the car?" would never have erased the damage.

Nothing is ever accomplished by wild anger. It is completely futile to let anger control you. It might have felt good, for a second or two, to yell at Laurie and release some tension, but what good would that have done? Is the portrait of a screaming, hysterical mother the one I want her to carry into adulthood? Do I want her to picture her growing-up time at home as a period of failures, accidents, and mistakes with a yelling mother superimposed over it all?

Laurie knew I was angry, hurt, and just plain "sick" over that scratch, simply by the look on my face. All I said was a quiet, "Oh, Laurie." Nothing more was needed. Losing my temper like an immature sore loser would have never given me the elaborate, sincere, heartfelt apology from Laurie the next day. The biggest victory comes though, when you realize that if you are angry at the problem and not the person, you are free from that hard knot of anger usually located in the pit of your stomach on days like that. (No Excedrin headaches, either.)

God knows there will be days when we will experience anger. There will even be days when we will fail to be in control of that anger (like the two experiences with my father). But He knows that if He can channel our anger we will be healthier, freer, and wiser.

God is careful to warn us about potential danger in anger. The Bible states, "Be ye angry and sin not" (Eph. 4:26). Watch out for that personal kind of anger—that's usually the kind we sin over. Then, direct your anger to the problem—not to the person.

If you are a woman whose life constantly displays the illness of chronic hostilities, you are suffering I know, but suffering needlessly. It isn't fatal, and it isn't too late for the cure. You have a temperament, we all do, but you can live without a temper. Read these wise, healing words of Paul.

If you are angry, be sure it is not out of wounded pride or bad temper [*Personal anger*]. Never go to bed angry, don't give the devil that sort of foothold. Let there be no more resentment, no more anger, or temper, no more violent self-assertiveness, no more slander and no more malicious remarks [*More personal anger*]. Be kind to each other; be understanding. Be as ready to forgive others as God for Christ's sake has forgiven you (Eph. 4:26,27,31,32 Phillips).

The portrait of you which your children should carry into adulthood is described in the last sentences. Will their picture of you be one of kindness, understanding, and forgiveness?

The whole world is looking longingly for this kind of beautiful woman. They are sick to death with the hatred and anger written across the faces of most people today.

God's woman has a fantastic source of beauty right at her elbow. She has a master cosmetologist beside her to erase the hard lines of anger. With a touch of His hand, He can soften her rigid skin into the beautiful flawless complexion of kindness. He rejuvenates her cheek bones by gently brushing them with the fresh glow of understanding. Her mouth glistens with the ointment of gentleness. He lets the inner fire of her soul add extra sparkle to her eyes, and they are bright with forgiveness. When He is finished with His work, He sends her out into the world He made, turns the floodlights up, and we all see *she is a beauty*.

Your eyes light up your inward being. A pure eye lets sunshine into your soul. A lustful eye shuts out the light and plunges you into darkness. So watch out that the sunshine isn't blotted out. If you are filled with light within, with no dark corners, then your face will be radiant too, as though a flood-light is beamed upon you (Luke 11:34-36).

Additional Verses:

		Colossians 3:5-10
Our behavior:	1 Corinthians 16:4	Proverbs 10:19
	2 Corinthians 6:3,4	Proverbs 12:16
	Ephesians 5:15-17	Proverbs 18:1,2
	1 John 3:18	Proverbs 28:13
	Proverbs 10:14	Proverbs 29:22

CHAPTER NINE

THE GRACIOUS BEAUTY OF FORGIVENESS AND LOVE

I know of an angry woman, such as I've described in the previous chapter, who lived out each day of her life in anger. She had accepted Christ many years back but had never grown in the Lord or kept her personal relationship to Him clear and open. She allowed little sins (nothing ever bigger than a white lie or a mini-gossip session) to pile up year after year. By the time she was in her mid-forties, she was a disaster to be around. We wondered how her husband put up with it.

She displayed all the symptoms of the angry out-of-the-right-relationship-with-God person. She had few (if any) real friends, no outside-the-home interests (no inside the home interests, either); so all of her attention was focused inwardly on herself. She was full of the poor-me attitude in public, and nagged her husband to death in private. (I should say, "semi-private" because we got in on a few remarks one night at dinner with them.)

Then, suddenly, almost over night, she changed.

My, how she changed! She was a different person and was a delight to be around.

I am told that after years of his wife's nagging, haranguing, arguing, and tongue lashing, the husband had turned to her one day and said, "What exactly is it that I have done to cause you to be this way? I must be responsible for at least part of your angry outbursts, so please tell me. I'd like to stop doing that to you."

His wife listened in stunned silence, and then wept as he said, "Will you forgive me for what I've done to you? Will you forgive me for failing to be the husband I should have been to you?"

When the wife was faced with such forgiving, loving kindness, she melted. She also got a clear look at the basic problem, which was not her husband and his faults, but herself.

If you have just guessed that the opposite of anger is forgiveness, you have guessed correctly. If you go one step further, you will realize that when anger and hate are dissolved by forgiveness, real loving is free to begin!

The woman who heard her husband's genuine request for forgiveness had to go back to her own forgiveness from God and begin again. God then began (overnight) to change her.

If there was a formula for making the Landorf marriage work after we became Christians, it began with my incredible realization that I was allowing the sin of anger to spew forth daily in my life. *I* was completely responsible for the anger in our marriage and for a good many ugly responses that came from Dick.

After my forgiveness for sins came from God, I sought out Dick's forgiveness. I said, "Will you forgive me for all those angry past failures? I do so want to be the perfect wife!"

(Just recently, when I was not doing overly well in the "perfect wife" department, Dick encouraged me with, "Joyce, I've got to hand it to you; you do try harder than anybody I know!")

Nothing melts angry resentments like the question, "Will you forgive me?" There is a warm current of strength running through those four words. There is also an honest humility about this question that pours over our souls and soothes like some fragrant balm.

Once, when I was speaking to some Army troops in Thailand, I was talking about asking this forgiving kind of question and I said, "Maybe someone right here needs to write a letter home to a mother, wife, or friend and ask, 'Will you forgive me?'"

I was somewhat startled by a soldier on the front row directly in front of me, who shot his hand in the air and said, "Excuse me, Ma'am, but I've got to say something. You're talking about me. It's me who's got to write that letter. Wait till I tell you!" He told how his wife and he were ready to get a divorce. Every letter he'd received from her had sent him to his pad of paper to fire off one angry page after another back to her. The last letter he had received from his wife arrived that morning and he had been waiting all day to write her one dandy, final sign-off letter.

His buddy had convinced him to come to my evening meeting at the chapel. He had sat there all through the music part of my performance just stewing over the letter he was going to write. But as I began to talk, the Lord started revealing to him the real cause of his problem. As he began to form some definite conclusions, he simply had to interrupt me. He was just beautiful as he said, "I've got to write her; I've got to ask her forgiveness. So many of our problems are my fault, not hers. I never saw that before. I've got to get right with God, too. It's been a long time since I've asked His forgiveness!"

He said some more things, but I couldn't see him because of my tears, and I couldn't hear him because of the joyous bells that were ringing and clanging in my ears.

Some of us have never tried asking for forgiveness. Oh, we've said, "I'm sorry," but we've said it without truthful conviction to enforce it. We are too proud, too stubborn, or too sure it won't work, and we refuse to see our responsibility in the situation.

Others of us have never seen that we have any fault or blame for the problem. We need desperately to confess our faults one to another and then, by God's grace, ask, "Will you forgive me?"

I am acutely aware that asking forgiveness and forgiving others is not easy. The guidelines and principles for forgiveness are not easily learned. It's far easier to practice them once and then forget them. Forgiveness must be kept up to date, and, when it is, life takes on new and different dimensions every day. It will take every ounce of energy and brains you've got to keep your marriage and your children growing. You will never run out of occasions to use these guidelines; new opportunities arise all the time. I do know, however, from experience, that these principles can be applied and they *do work*.

A woman can muddle through her problems feeling angry and confused. She can suffer as a victim of "terrible circumstances." She can "live through" her problems. But I recommend "loving through" instead. You can love your way through confusion into peace. You can learn to understand the real issues in life. You can even understand yourself in these issues.

Here are the guidelines, and I pray they will be helpful and practical to you.

1. *Realize you cannot change some things.*

The woman who has let anger rob her of her beauty is most easily identified by the way she *pounces*.

She pounces on relatives, mate, children, past events and future events faster than you can blink an eye. She critically pounces on any unobtainable or unrealistic goals in her life or yours. Heaven help you if you have a wart on your nose, because she loves to pounce on a person's physical characteristics.

The woman of forgiveness sees the same problems, the same people, and even the same wart. Yet, she makes up her mind to accept them all. There are just a great number of things, people, and circumstances that cannot be changed. The woman of beauty accepts things which cannot be altered, and she accepts them *without* a martyr complex. She can be sensitive and alert to the needs of others because she has known God's forgiveness and love in those same areas of her life.

Most of us are willing to accept a person's good traits. Few of us are willing to look at and love a person with all his or her traits. You may not be able to change

> your husband's stubbornness (or his snoring).
> your son's acne (or his messy room).
> your daughter's height (or her love of old jeans).
> your mother-in-law's set ways (or her remarks).
> your parents' attitudes (or lack of attitudes).
> your financial problems (except by burning your credit cards).
> your physical disabilities (or your new bifocals).

So why bother? Remember this famous prayer?

> God, grant me the serenity
> To accept the things I cannot change,
> Courage to change the things I can,
> And the wisdom to know the difference.

It's highly possible that God will not change certain people in your life. He may not take away problems, but, if He doesn't, don't be discouraged. He will give you the relaxed grace to accept them, to live with them, and even to love them. (Read 2 Cor. 12:9. It's a promise!)

Henrietta Mears often said, "I believe my greatest spiritual asset throughout my entire life has been my failing sight for it has kept me absolutely dependent on God!" (*Henrietta Mears and How She Did It*, cited previously) Now that is a beautiful woman! She has accepted her loss, and she is grateful for it, because it keeps her in the right relationship with God.

2. *Realize you will have differences.*

I worry just a little when a couple confidently states, "We *never* have an argument." All this really says is that (1) they are lying, or (2) one of them has given up all his or her rights, ideas, opinions, and thoughts.

Someone pulled our son aside a few years back and whispered, "Tell me the truth, now, do your mommy and daddy ever have fights or arguments?" Rick said he didn't think so. He answered honestly because Dick and I don't have knock-down, drag-out fights (as we used to) but we do have conflicts. Our method of handling them has changed from my radical screaming at Dick to my quietly saying, "Oh, Hon, I've got to talk about something with you, O.K.?"

We all tend to presume that so-and-so doesn't have arguments or conflicts in his life. We are especially sure of that if so-and-so is named Billy Graham or if he is a minister or missionary. (Even some authors are accused of "having it made.") We must stop putting people (even "spiritual giants") on pedestals, because they are human and they *do have conflicts*.

Because each of us is uniquely different, we will always have some areas of disagreement. We may even have outright conflicts, but we no longer need to scream our vengeance or run away from our problems.

Not long ago, I was hurt by a remark Dick had repeated four times in my presence. The old Joyce would have let everyone there know the truth. I would have charged in to "right" every wrong by explaining everything. The forgiven Joyce asked God for perfect timing, a clean heart, and a right spirit. Later, when the time came, I told Dick I was hurt and that I knew it was silly of me, but I wanted to talk about our differences. (It would have been easier to have swept the whole thing under the rug and not mention it. But I know from experience that if I did that, I'd sneak back every day, lift up the rug, and poke around in the dirt.)

After Dick and I had talked over the minor problem and worked out a solution, we found our love quota had gone up many points. Our relationship is always stronger after these workouts, but it starts with admitting there is a difference of opinion and then doing something about it.

The wise woman of beauty waits for God's timing, and then privately discusses the issues. She does not ridicule or even poke the digging type of humor at her husband in front of children, friends, or associates. She applies the same principle of privacy when she deals with her children's conflicts, whenever it's possible. And, most important, she attacks the problems, not the people. The wise woman of beauty accepts the challenge of reconciliation, and she becomes an expert in this next step.

3. *Resolve differences creatively.*

David Augsburger said,

"Resolving conflict creatively is the result of love-in-action. Love is something you do. It must be expressed in all three levels of communication: the verbal (I love you), the nonverbal (I feel with you, I truly hear you), and the symbolic (I give to you)."*

The ugly woman does not want to bother with settling anything creatively. She is too self-centered to want to take the time, effort, and thought that creative living costs. It's easier to just blow up, to say what's on her mind. She stands by and lets the chips fall where they may. She feels a bit guilty afterwards but justifies her words and angry actions by saying, "Well, I can forgive so-and-so but I'll never forget. After all, look what *he did* to me!"

The woman who would solve the daily problems and differences in her life by using a creative method is very beautiful.

I asked one such beauty, Pat French, about her temper and if she had one. "Very definitely, but it's under control," she answered. I asked her how that had been accomplished in her life. This, as accurately as I can recall, was her answer:

Cherishable: Love and Marriage, Herald Press, Scottdale, Pa., 1971.

"All my life has been filled with problems. The Lord has allowed me to experience every kind of problem and trial imaginable. Never once, at any time or in any way, has another human being been able to solve those problems. No one has come up with any solutions. So, for a long time, now I've gone only to the Lord with my troubles. He is the only one capable of solving things. I take my anger over a person or a problem immediately to the Lord. I tell Him I've no one but Him, and He in turn gives me the control I need for that moment."

Then, thoughtfully, she added later, "You know, I suspect that a good many Christian women are too sheltered from real problems, so they've developed no spiritual muscles. They are too weak and powerless to cope with problems. They really don't believe God can help, but oh, He can and does."

If only Christian women would think of their problems as spiritual muscle builders, we'd have churches full of strong, vibrant, healthy women. Homes would be filled with the savory aroma of forgiveness and love, and we'd see faces glowing from the exquisite beauty of God's love.

"Yes, Joyce," you say, "but what you are saying is not so easily done. It's hard to be forgiving and loving."

That's right, it *is* hard. But who said it would be easy? Who said that if you become a Christian you automatically become an expert in loving? Not me!

Peter gave us a clue as to how it's done when he said, "Now you can have real love for everyone because your souls have been cleansed from selfishness and hatred when you trusted Christ to save you; so see to it that you really do love each other warmly, with all your hearts" (1 Peter 1:22).

He gave two points for loving. Remember you've been forgiven, and then see to it that you love! (Back to "Make up your mind, Lady!")

But none of this is easily, or naturally done. In fact,

the forgiving kind of loving will cost you a great deal. It may cost you everything you have.

It's very expensive and time consuming ...

To apologize.
To begin all over again.
To be unselfish.
To take advice.
To admit error.
To face criticism.
To be charitable to the ungrateful.
To keep on trying.
To be considerate.
To appreciate him or her.
To avoid mistakes.
To make allowances for others.
To bear a personal insult.
To believe the best about someone.
To endure success.
To profit by mistakes.
To forgive by Christ's love and forget.
To think and then to act.
To keep out of the rut.
To grow older.
To make the best of little things.
To maintain high standards.
To understand someone's thoughtless blunder.
To shoulder deserved blame.
To subdue impulsive anger.
To recognize a person's worth.
To see the silver lining.
To let the beauty of Christ be seen.

You see, these are expensive, costly things because it is not easy or cheap to love—*but it always pays!*

The world would have us believe that the greatest power known to man is force. The Lord has proven that the greatest force in the world is love. Love, His love, never fails. Have you seen it working in your face, your life, your home?

Our daughter, Laurie, has always been cute and perky! She's charmed everyone for years with her darling, yet surprising personality. But now that she is almost 18, she has turned into a smashing beauty. She was not always so shimmering with loveliness. I recall somewhere in her fourteenth year, she had her own rebellion about everything from skirt lengths to hating peas and carrots. She made it very difficult for us to love her, and she casually, yet deliberately, drove us all up the wall! She didn't go into drugs (four friends did). She didn't have an abortion (one friend did). But for 18 months she doubted everything about the Lord, she disagreed with everything we said or did, and she made life in general miserable. We refused to let any of her ugly actions stop our loving her—it wasn't easy but we managed in spite of her.

Just when I was beginning to think we'd never see the end of this angry rebellion, she had her own experience with the Lord. (God has no *grand*children.) I had insisted that she go on tour with our church high school choir. She reluctantly went, and the first night changed her life forever. She was angry and mad at everyone from God on down to herself and everyone in between. But she was mostly fed up with herself, so she prayed, OK, Lord, if You can be real, be real to me!"

God's bolt of lightning struck her, dead center, and she came home a changed girl. It took us six months to adjust to the new Laurie. I almost fainted when she came into my kitchen that first night home and said, "Oh, Mom, everything smells so wonderful! What's for dinner?"

I thank God that none of her mean traits, ugly ways, or rebellious actions convinced us to stop loving her or praying for her, because what we now have is *something else!*

I've seen this forgiving, loving power of God work a lasting miracle in Laurie's life. There is a joyous, radiant spirit shining like a halo around her head. It was best described by a boy, named Mark, when he came to pick up Laurie for a date recently.

She was still getting ready, so Mark was chatting with me. He was in some involved explanation about something when the hall door opened and Laurie came through.

She was quite a picture. Her blonde hair was softly curled around her shoulders, her blue eyes were sparkling, and her slim size-seven figure was a delight to see. Mark took her all in and stopped mid-sentence. No one moved, then he said very quietly, "Wow, Laurie, you look so soft . . ."

I've thought of that moment many times, because she did, indeed, look so soft, so gentle, and so lovely. I couldn't help but compare the old Laurie to the new Laurie. I remembered how anger had made her almost cruel looking at times. How hard her eyes had looked, but not any more. Not now, because of the gentle, softening action of God's forgiveness and love.

God's love never fails. Its softening ability is one of the biggest contributions to beauty a woman can experience. Have you seen it? It's a thing of beauty and a joy forever.

Additional Verses:

Accept life:

Psalm 13:5, 6
Psalm 37:1-9
Psalm 15
James 5:16

New life:

Colossians 3:12-14
James 1:19-21
James 1:26

Try love, you'll like it:

1 Peter 2:1-4
1 Peter 4:8
Romans 12:9, 10
1 John 3:14-16
1 John 3:18
1 John 4:18, 19
James 4:11

Future benefits of loving: Psalm 22:30
                              Psalm 25:12, 13
                              Psalm 37:25, 26

CHAPTER TEN

YOU AND YOUR BEAUTIFUL PERSONALITY

The rain alternates its sound level from a light drizzling patter to the heavy plopping drops of a downpour, but other than that, my house is quiet. I'm writing this in my warm, comfortable living room, surrounded by books, papers, notes, and clippings.

I can't help but wish that for this last chapter I could see you, talk with you, and wrap up this book with you—face to face.

There never seems to be enough time for that sort of thing, and I suppose it's unrealistic to think I could crowd you all into my living room, anyway. But I wish I could.

A few times in my life I've been able to do just that with a friend. Like some special times with Clare (the beautiful woman to whom this book is dedicated), when over a steaming cup of hot tea we have sat and shared, in the language of love, our thoughts about life in our world. Those times though, have been rare because of the schedules and the busyness of our lives.

Since the days of our ancestors, our busy pace has steadily increased. By now, we all whirl so much we need somebody (sometimes anybody) to stop the whirling. We need to hold still for a minute and reflect on our beginnings. We need to share with someone some of the puzzling mysteries of our lives and personalities.

Nowadays, there are no pot-bellied stoves in country stores where we can voice our opinion loud and strong. There are few, if any, quilting bees held in small church circles where we can make small talk or trade confidences. There are some small group meetings after church and some small prayer groups, but not nearly enough to handle the need for developing the personality God would want for us.

I don't really believe there is such a thing as a self-made man (or woman). We need people. We need to develop, and to do that we need to converse with each other.

Strangely, though, there doesn't seem to be enough time for the founding and nurturing of a slow, steady friendship with someone who shares our ideals, backgrounds, and concerns.

We seem to live out our lives as spectators at a drama called *life*. Our fellowman is so inventive, he has besieged us with so much to entertain us, that even the art of conversation has lost most of its sparkle.

Women don't enjoy other women basically because of two things relating to conversation: (1) meaningless prattling small talk and (2) destructive, negative discussions. Even prayer meeting can be a disguised trap. We hear a lady request prayer and she says, "We must pray for Joanne because—well, you know—she's having marital problems." (As a matter-of-fact, I didn't know, and my mind doesn't hear the next request because I'm still back on Joanne wondering "*What* marital problems?")

Or women meet in masses at various supermarkets, big parties, large churches, P.T.A., or women's meetings, and there's only time enough for a brief greeting.

"Did you have a good summer?"

"It seems like ages since I saw you last."

"I don't know where the time goes."

"I've been meaning to call you but. . . ."

The meaningless words rush and tumble out, and we only have time for top thoughts, hurried hands with quick pats, and hidden hearts. Subjects are lightly touched. Emotions are labeled "sentimentality," and any prying beneath the surface is branded as bad manners.

So it is, that in our day we don't know very much about anybody; and, conversely, nobody knows very much about us. What's worse, however, is that we know precious little about ourselves!

Once there was a time when we spread ourselves, our thoughts, and our dreams around. We let off steam here, there, and everywhere, at least now and then. But now, that's not quite the thing to do. In fact, we are not too sure we have any steam any more. But we do! We have steam, we have emotions, and we even have hopes and dreams.

Human nature does not change. Yet, somewhere over the years the doors through which we used to walk freely into each other's hearts and minds have been shut—closed tight.

There is much in us that is wonderful and awful, good and bad, which we do not understand and which we do not talk about. We presume no one ever had our peculiar problem so we keep the scalding steam of inner conflicts all bottled up, and it has no place to blow off.

I remember, during my childhood, my father's church had the practice of the "open altar." After the meeting, the altar area was open for anyone to come, kneel, pray, cry, or just be silent before the Lord. (My dearest memories are of my mother kneeling, praying, and crying before the Lord.) Somewhere along the path of growing up, I lost the open altar concept and closed all channels of sharing with God or friend.

Now, out of our modern age and symbolic of it, has come a new highly specialized science. It's called psychiatry.

"Psychiatry," states William Glasser, "must be concerned with two basic psychological needs; (1) the need to love and be loved and (2) the need to feel that we are worthwhile to ourselves and others."*

*Reality Therapy, Harper and Row, New York, N.Y.

Careful, conscientious men and women are practicing this new science. Christian psychologists and psychiatrists are among my dearest friends and co-workers, and I can rejoice over the results of their dedicated work.

These gifted, listening people have helped some women to work things out for themselves. Many a woman has been given direction in figuring out where and when conflicts began in her life. Often, when a woman can mentally work and figure things out, she frees herself from the frustrations of life that would keep her shut up as an emotional invalid.

Sometimes, though, in spite of a psychologist's, psychiatrist's, or counselor's dedicated efforts, we find a woman who just cannot accept healing. Other women won't go to a Christian doctor to begin with. Still others won't even admit there is a problem, so God's healing hand cannot cure them. Why?

My mother once gave me an illustration to help with this difficult "why." It went like this. Your watch breaks, so you take it to a master watch repair specialist. He carefully takes your watch apart, spreads it on the work bench before you, and gives his show-and-tell lesson on why it doesn't work. The rusty spring here, the clogged and dirty wheel here, and a broken mainspring there are just a few of the problems. Slowly he cleans, mends, oils, replaces parts, and puts it all together again. He finishes and hands your old watch back to you, not new, but repaired.

Now, see if you understand this comparison. In the rush of life, your world breaks down and threatens to quit running altogether, so you take it to someone who has studied the conflicts of living. He spreads out your rusty emotions, your clogged-up sinful life, and your broken dreams on the table before you. But then, differing from the watch repairman, he says, "Now, here's where you went wrong. All you have to do is pick up the pieces and put your life back into running order. I'll help you all I can, but you must do it by yourself." He gives you all sorts of encouragement but, somehow, you just can't do it. You know you need something more . . . what? You can't say . . . but it's just *something* else. (I know this from experience, because I've sat at the same table.)

Fifteen years ago I had nobody to talk to, though I was surrounded with people who loved me and whom I loved. I would not go to a psychologist or counselor. I couldn't confide my inner conflicts in my best friend, my husband, or my parents without tearing them down to my own level. I was sure they wouldn't understand my conflicts, or, worse, they would judge me for them. I was supposed to be a strong person, whether I wanted to be or not. A good psychologist could have pointed out the beginnings, the early, basic warning signs and the main spots of my conflicts, but I'm not sure it would have been an answer for me. I could not cope with anything.

You see, even after I'd intellectually figured things out, seen where I'd gone wrong, analyzed the problems in my past life and background, I *still* did not have any answers. To try and put the pieces of my life back together again was a cruel joke, an impossibility.

Many difficult emotions built up, and then increased, and finally multiplied. There was not room enough inside me, just as there is not room enough inside any of us, for all the terrors, the troubles, the longings, and the dreams. They have to spill over somewhere and on someone.

By the time I chose suicide as the only option left open to me, I had intellectually figured it all out, but had no cure and no real answers. I didn't know I had to establish a joint enterprise with God for the lasting cure.

The answers to life's conflicts do not come from another friend, doctor, or counselor.

If you are to spread your thoughts, your dreams, your unacknowledged wickedness, your passing crazy fantasies, your hopes, your loves and hates out on a table, like pieces of a watch before a repair man, you must do it before Someone who has within Him greater tolerance, greater comprehension and supernatural powers of forgiveness. There is only one such person and that is GOD.

Fifteen years ago, because of a phone call, I was stopped during the act of suicide; and alone, I went before God. To my amazement, He heard me.

He was the Master Designer who spread the pieces of my life out on the table, explaining the conflicts as He went along. Then, unlike the watch repair man or the doctor, He wiped the pieces off the table with one sweeping motion, and said, tenderly, "Here, dear broken and battered child, take this. It's your new life—whole and complete. I did not come to patch and glue you back together again, but I've come to bring you a new life. I'll keep the wheels of your soul oiled with forgiveness; I'll wind the mainspring of your thoughts with My love; and you will live and tick away the seconds of this life with great hope, peace, and abundant joy!"

All our strength to live comes from being in a joint enterprise with God. There is always an answer to life's conflicts. Psychologists can play an important part in helping us to see the troubled areas, but if your doctor does not ultimately point you to the all forgiving God, then you may never be cured. No doctor in the world can resolve the sin-caused conflicts within you. He can only point you in God's direction. It is God alone who can forgive.

A beautiful, openly honest personality begins with acknowledging our need and opening our minds, wills, and emotions to the God of answers. It may mean finding your own "open altar," kneeling before Him, and praying.

> Dear God,
> Here I am, problems and all. Forgive me. Forgive my sins. I'm worn out, broken, and I can't be patched up. I need a new life. Please come into my soul and touch me with Your healing hands. I want to exchange

my hates for Your loves.

my anger for your forgiveness.

my insecurities for Your high evaluations.

my worry for Your words in prayer.

my fear for a measure of Your fadeless faith.

my bitterness for Your thanksgiving.

Now, thank You, Lord, for doing all this, even before I see change or results. Amen.

The woman who prays this and accepts God's forgiveness has connected her spirit with God's. She has entered into a joint enterprise with the God who made her.

Her personality begins to show some special traits and spiritual qualities. The inner beauteous glow begins.

1. *She has a sense of spiritual things.*

She does not merely quote Bible truths, she transforms them into solid realities. Her daily reading of God's Word teaches her the fine art of Christian living. When she listens to you, she sees you as Christ would see you. When you look closely, you see she glows with the gift of peace. Jesus said, "I am leaving you with a gift—peace of mind and heart! And the peace I give isn't fragile like the world gives. So don't be troubled or afraid" (John 14:27).

2. *She has a sense of indescribable sweetness about her.*

This is not a saccharine, phony sweetness but a genuine one. When you talk with her, you feel the presence of the altogether lovely One, and you know He is dear to her. She is like my beautiful friend, Dale Evans Rogers; actress, singer, and author, who was asked rather rudely if she'd had a surgical face lift. Dale just answered sweetly, "No, no face lift—just my heart."

3. *She has a sense of victory over temptations.*

She very definitely admits to having temptations—big and small, but she has made up her mind to be habitually triumphant over them. She has taken the wise counsel of Paul to her heart and mind. He said, "I advise you to obey the Holy Spirit's instructions. He will tell you where to go and what to do, and then you won't always be doing the wrong things your evil nature wants you to do" (Gal. 5:16).

4. *She has a sacred sense of concern for others.*

Because of the nearness and presence of Jesus in her life, she develops the God-given urge to share Him with others. She longs to reveal salvation's answers of love for living with all whom she meets. She has the mind of Christ in her thoughts. Imagine the joy of thinking His thoughts and revealing His love to others! She knows the beauty of the words in Acts 20:24, "But life is worth nothing unless I use it for doing the work assigned me by the Lord Jesus—the work of telling others [in her home, her neighborhood, even her P.T.A.] the Good News about God's mighty kindness and love."

5. *She shows a great sense of spiritual power.*

She does not fear people—individually or in groups. She knows the Holy Spirit's power is at work within her. She carries out her duties with a delightful disposition, but she is quietly dynamic with power. Talk about a beauty—she's one! Can you see her? Do you know someone like her?

We can all be radiantly beautiful if we care to try. When Christ lives within us, we have these foregoing five senses at our beck and call. We don't have to live with passive, colorless personalities. We can accept God's forgiveness and claim His benefits. We can begin to really relate to people. We can live as we've never lived before. Our personalities can be enhanced beyond our fondest hopes. (God is quite a specialist in this department!)

When a woman really trusts Christ and believes what God has to say about her "oneness" with Him, her old personality drops off like a rotten garment. Every faculty of her being seems to be energized anew by the Holy Spirit.

Paul really described what we could be like with the Holy Spirit's power working in our lives when he wrote, "But when the Holy Spirit controls our lives,

He will produce this kind of fruit in us: love, joy, peace, patience, kindness, faithfulness, gentleness, and self-control. . . . If we are living now by the Holy Spirit's power, let us follow the Holy Spirit's leading in every part of our lives. Then we won't need to look for honors and popularity which lead to jealousy and hard feelings" (Gal. 5:22, 23, 25, 26).

The beautiful woman whose life shows the fruit of the Spirit, exhibits some other practical qualities as well. They are the qualities that make her personality real and down to earth.

1. *She has the fragrance of humor.*

She might not have been born with a great sense of humor, but she trains her mind to look at her life's happenings in good humor. She keeps her perspective. When she is a young wife and mother, she can smile (and even cope) during dinner's chaotic routine with little children. She is able to project a picture of herself in her mind's eye of a few years later when she will have no small children to spill their milk or ask her to cut up their meat. She can see herself in the years to come when the children have gone, and she is not afraid. She will warm herself by memories' fire and recall a thousand dinners, by their fun giggling, outright laughter and special "in" family jokes.

She will not take her life too seriously but will continually train herself to find the humor in it.

Her good sense of humor has helped her to take the three steps to real living which Peter talks about in 2 Peter 1:6-8. (1) "Learn to put aside your own desires so that you will become patient and godly, gladly letting God have his way with you. This will make possible the next step, (2) which is for you to enjoy other people and to like them, and finally (3) you will grow to love them deeply. The more you go on in this way, the more you will grow strong spiritually and become fruitful and useful to our Lord Jesus Christ."

2. *She has the fragrance of friendship.*

"A cheerful heart does good like medicine, but a broken spirit makes one sick" (Prov. 17:22).

"Some women just make me sick," you've heard people say, and I'm sure it's because the women they refer to do not know how to be friendly. The friendly woman greets you with a warm smile whether she knows you or not!

She recognizes the tremendous therapeutic value of a smile to her husband and to her children. (Most husbands need a "buffer zone" between their work and their home. Some stop at a bar for a few drinks. Others drive home—*very slowly*.) The beautiful woman prepares herself and her children for his arrival. She greets him in friendliness. Her spirit of friendship is motivated by the principle of Galatians 6:10, where we read,

"Whenever we can we should always be kind to everyone, and especially to our Christian brothers."

3. *She has the fragrance of organization.*

She does not have this fanatic *thing* about cleanliness and being neat and tidy always. She does not drive anyone up a wall over a speck of dirt, but *she is neat.* Her house, according to the present rate of speed of their family life, has a semblance of order. She is not a slave chained to the mop, pail, and scrub brush, but her house is no cluttered, dirty, pigpen either. She's sure God does not want her to live in an unorganized mess of a house. (Nor is she a grooming disaster.)

The beautiful woman concentrates on her corner of the world and, while there, does her very best, as Scripture exhorts. "Let everyone be sure that he [or she] is doing his [or her] very best, for then he [or she] will have the personal satisfaction of work well done, and won't need to compare himself [or herself] with someone else" (Gal. 6:4).

4. *She has the fragrance of hospitality.*

She opens her home to others even when her couch is rather threadbare, the walls need paint, and she doesn't have enough dishes or chairs. She shares her dinner table, without apologies, and can be gracious even if it's only "hamburger night." She makes you feel that you have added the special magic ingredient to an evening just by being there. She never says, "Can I getcha something?" She says, "Let's see, I have the hot water going—which will it be, coffee or tea?"

If you drop in on her unexpectedly, you take her (and her house) as is, and instantly she puts you at ease. She may say, "Good grief, I look awful, but come in; pardon the mess. How good to see you!" No apologies follow after that, and her hospitality remains a warm memory for a long time to come.

The fragrance of hospitality is enhanced by her concern involving the social graces.

Etiquette is no dirty nine-letter word to her. She practices and teaches manners as routinely as she practices and teaches Bible truths. She knows "etiquette" is just another name for being kind to one another. (Many Christian families have forgotten that being kind to each other happens to be one of the secondary themes running the length of the New Testament.) She has privately sought for (and received) her husband's cooperation in this venture. (Nothing teaches children to chew food with their mouths closed quite like a mother and father who chew food with their mouths closed!)

She does many things in the spirit of hospitality, but we rarely find out about them for she has heeded Jesus' admonition, "Take care! Don't do your good deeds publicly, to be admired, for then you will lose the reward from your Father in heaven. But when you do a kindness to someone, do it secretly—don't tell your left hand what your right hand is doing" (Matt. 6:1, 3).

This practice of doing good in secret adds the clearest of twinkles to her already sparkling eyes!

5. *She has the fragrance of wonder.*

Nothing is too small or insignificant to catch her attention. She is interested in everything. She teaches her children the sense of wonder by pointing out the little brown bug on the ground, the sleeping kitty, and the orange sunset. She works at keeping their natural wonder alive. She, herself, is so filled with wonder she becomes an interesting, colorful person. She smiles and talks with her eyes, and her face lights up over the wonder of little things. She is a joy to see.

6. *She has the fragrance of honesty.*

She does not lie—even about little things. If she is busy and does not want to answer her phone, she does not say to her children, "Tell them Mommie is not home." She says, "Tell them Mommie is busy and will call them back later." She teaches them honesty in the best of ways—by example.

Shortly after my friend Clare became a Christian, she was deeply convicted about a note she'd sent to school for her children's absences. She had claimed illness for their absence when actually they had gone on a short vacation.

After the Lord dealt with her about it and her pride was leveled a bit, she wrote a letter to the principal saying she'd lied and explaining that since she was now a Christian she wanted to right the wrong.

The principal read it as Clare stood there (another leveling moment) and then thoughtfully said, "In all the years I've been at this job, I've read thousands of excuse notes. Hundreds of them have been outright lies. This is the *very first* letter of confession I've ever received."

A beautiful woman doesn't lie about her age. She doesn't even have to hide how old she is. She's learned that all she really has to call her own is the moment she is living right now. She takes the years as they come. To her, each succeeding year is the best. She has accepted the fact that she is not one minute older or younger than God wants her to be! Because she doesn't lie about her age, God ages her gracefully.

Most Christian women rarely face the fact that they can and do lie. Not this beautiful gal who wrote,

Oh, yes, by the way, Joyce, just last week I discovered a terrible thing I do—I tell little lies! Oh, how shocking the hard faced truth of that was! Imagine after all these years of doing it and defending it [we usually justify the lie because our motives are good] I now see it as a sin—through God's eyes. I almost jumped out of my car seat when I saw and realized this. So, I confessed my lies, and I'm so happy. I've actually consistently begun telling the truth. In fact, I've had one whole week where I didn't tell one single lie—what a victory. It feels great!

(I *know* the feeling—praise God!)

7. *She has the fragrance of learning*

She is not afraid to develop new skills. She tries to do something creative at least once a day—even if it's only adding a dash of paprika and parsley to her mashed potatoes. She reads a wide range of books. She takes instruction, from a Bible study course to needlepoint classes. She is enthusiastically dedicated to increasing her learning powers and her willingness to tackle a new project is gorgeous!

8. *She has the fragrance of balanced priorities.*

The beautiful woman is one who has asked God about the goals and priorities of her life, and He has opened several new doors. First, she found she is a person—a woman—she is somebody! Then, she discovered, by much praying, God's highly original list of what's-up-first for her life. The truly lovely woman does not want to be a carbon copy of even the most beautiful woman, but wants to be what God wants *her* to be. Some women can't handle marriage, child raising, and a job simultaneously. Others manage the whole bit with astonishing perfection. God deals individually with each of us, and what He may do in your life, He may not do in mine. If a woman keeps her check-list of priorities handy, she will be fragrant with the originality God has planned for her.

9. *She has the fragrance of appreciation.*

She knows that in life the essence of appreciation is like butter on the toast: it makes it go down much easier. She has sincere thankfulness running through her veins. It is not the phony or gushy put-on type but a real, appropriate sense of appreciation. She has days when she does not feel thankful (especially for an illness or at the death of a loved one), but she understands the nature of a God-allowed crisis. She knows God uses crises to develop and mature character. She does not resent problems because she understands their work in her life. Whether she sees the results of being thankful or not, she knows God can be trusted.

She is not only obediently thankful, but also scatters seeds of genuine praise to everyone around her. Long after they have left a gathering, she says to her husband, "Oh, Hon, you said a beautiful thing tonight about so-and-so. Thank you for being you."

In the quiet of her daughter's bedroom, she says, "Sweetie, when I saw you tonight, standing beside those other kids, my heart just swelled with pride because God gave you to me!"

When someone compliments her, she responds with *"thank you*—you've just made me feel so special."

She uses words to encourage and praise others, and the sound of her voice is the best sound in the world!

These nine fragrances are only a few of the truly beautiful woman's characteristics, but I pray you've caught the aroma and you're measuring and evaluating the fragrances of your own life.

The rain is still coming down, and I must close this book and lay aside my pen.

Just now I looked out our window and saw our pitiful rose garden. The rose bushes, poor darlings, are almost flooded out, and my husband has hurt their feelings and their stems by severely pruning them. They are not things of beauty at this moment. Not only are they pruned way back, but soon they will suffer the indignation of having their roots mulched. They will be sure the end is near. But it will get worse before it gets better because after their leaves start budding, my husband will spray them for aphids. Then the rose bushes will just know they'll never survive. But they will, and in a few short weeks, after they've been fed some special rose food, they will begin to have their first buds of bloom. These beauties will burst forth into full blossom in a glorious color that can only be described as "Shouting Pink." Since they are the Floribunda variety, they will grow in profusion. Rain or sun will not deter their efforts, and the fragrance—my, the fragrance—will just astound family and friends again this year.

The woman who has asked Christ into her life has the same fantastic potential for beauty as those rose bushes. She may not understand (or look forward to) the losses of the pruning season, but she knows pruning means growth, not death.

When her roots are disturbed, the change does not panic her. She looks to God for her strength. She feeds daily and regularly on His words, and her roots grow deep into the soil of His love.

When the stinging spray of disappointment washes over her soul, she knows the suffering is only temporary. She hangs onto her faith and is a little surprised because she feels growth through it all.

When the rain beats down on her, she accepts it as God's way of washing off the diseases of fear, worry, insecurity, anger, and bitterness. She holds her head high and thinks the thoughts of God.

She prepares her heart for blooming with a running conversation with God, and she is kept enthusiastic by His words.

She blossoms into the fragrant, colorful flower God has uniquely designed her to be.

She well knows her frailties, weak traits, and failures, but she also knows she is God's woman. She throbs with the bloom of life!

She knows that no matter how a woman fixes her face or her hair or takes care of her outer looks, if she has not Christ, she will have no real beauty. She will be like a flower with no perfume, no fragrance, no essence to remember.

The beautiful woman of God knows exactly who made her. She is an original design, and she is loved by her Maker.

Saint Augustine, in the Tenth Book of Confessions, wrote,

> I asked the earth and it answered,
> "I am not He,"
> and whatsoever are in it
> confessed the same.

> I asked the sea and the depths
> and the living, creeping things,
> and they answered,
> "We are not thy God.
> seek above us."

> I asked the moving air,
> the heavens, sun, moon and stars.
> "Nor, (say they) are we the God
> whom thou seekest."

> And I replied unto all things
> which encompass the door of my flesh,

> "Ye have told me of my God,
> that ye are not He;
> Tell me something of Him!"
> and they cried out with a loud voice,

> "He made us ... we are not God,
> *But He made us!*"

Just think of that, *He made us!*

The woman who understands the truth of who she is and why she's loved is completely surrounded by a fragrance. It is an unmistakable fragrance, swirling around her in a fine, penetrating mist. It is the real, the God-given fragrance of beauty!

This woman is what every Christ-centered woman can and should be ...

BEAUTIFUL, BEYOND WORDS!

Additional Verses:

Honesty:	Ephesians 4:15
Lying:	1 Peter 3:10
Resisting temptation:	1 Corinthians 10:13
	1 Peter 1:14
Thankfulness:	Proverbs 20:12
	1 Thessalonians 5:18
Attitudes:	Philippians 2:5-7
	Philippians 2:14-16
Obeying:	1 Peter 2:13
Needing others:	1 Corinthians 11:11
	1 Corinthians 12
	Genesis 2:23, 24
	Hebrews 10:25
Living:	Revelation 3:8

TITLES FOR CHRISTIAN WOMEN
all by Joyce Landorf

JOYCE, I FEEL LIKE I KNOW YOU Practical and Bible-based counsel on questions asked by women who approach Joyce Landorf with, "Joyce, I feel like I know you . . ." She answers questions on being lonely . . . being single . . . being divorced . . . being 14 and homely . . . and more. An excellent study for a women's only group. Textbook 6-2742—$2.25/Leader's Guide 6-2958—$1.25

THE FRAGRANCE OF BEAUTY You can be beautiful. Joyce Landorf tells you how, with God's help, the beauty in any woman can be released through her personality and her appearance. Deals with enemies to beauty such as fear . . . worry . . . inferiority. And looks at the practical benefits of faith . . . prayer . . . self-acceptance . . . forgiveness . . . thankfulness. An excellent study for women. Over 300,000 in print. Textbook 6-2231—$1.95/Leader's Guide 6-2912—$1.25

FOR THESE FRAGILE TIMES A beautiful gift book for those who are coming apart at the seams—bit by bit—or sometimes feel at though they are. A refreshing, warm, and understanding approach to living and trusting God—in the most shattering experiences. 6- 2805—$2.95

Prices subject to change.

Add 40¢ postage and handling for the first book, plus 10¢ for each additional book ordered. Add $1 minimum order service charge for orders less than $5.

Buy these titles at your local Christian bookstore or order from

VICTOR BOOKS

a division of SP Publications, Inc.
WHEATON, ILLINOIS 60187